IN CASE YOU FORGET

HANNAH R. CONWAY

Brentwood, Tennessee

To my daughters, Jadelyn and Willa.

I love you. Remember who you are and whose you are.
You are His. Hold tight to this truth forever,
and let it permeate every aspect of your lives.

Copyright ©·2023 by Hannah R. Conway
All rights reserved.
Printed in China

978-1-0877-7370-4

Published by B&H Publishing Group,
Brentwood, Tennessee

Dewey Decimal Classification: J242.62
Subject Heading: DEVOTIONAL LITERATURE / GIRLS / CHRISTIAN LIFE

Unless otherwise noted, Scripture quotations are taken from
the Christian Standard Bible®, Copyright © 2017 by Holman Bible
Publishers. Used by permission. Christian Standard Bible® and
CSB® are federally registered trademarks of Holman Bible Publishers.

1 2 3 4 5 6 7 • 27 26 25 24 23

Contents

Introduction 1

Week 1 3

Day 1: Made in God's Image

Day 2: Forgiven

Day 3: Pursued

Day 4: A Coheir

Day 5: Ruler

Day 6: Filled with Power

Day 7: Valuable

Week 2 25

Day 1: Adopted

Day 2: Eternally Royal

Day 3: Belong

Day 4: Rewarded

Day 5: On His Mind

Day 6: Free

Day 7: Prayed For

Week 3 47

Day 1: Planned

Day 2: Worth Saving

Day 3: A Disciple

Day 4: Gifted

Day 5: Known
Day 6: Provided For
Day 7: Seen and Heard

Week 4 69

Day 1: Liked
Day 2: Filled with Fruit
Day 3: A Temple
Day 4: An Influencer
Day 5: Alive
Day 6: Given Purpose
Day 7: Capable

Week 5 91

Day 1: Chosen
Day 2: Saved
Day 3: Comforted
Day 4: A Friend
Day 5: A Champion
Day 6: So Loved
Day 7: Enduring

Week 6 113

Day 1: Treasured
Day 2: Never Alone
Day 3: A New Creation
Day 4: A Kingdom Citizen
Day 5: Secure
Day 6: Unified
Day 7: Called and Commissioned

Introduction

The world has so much to say about who girls should be. Girls like you grow up hearing conflicting messages from social media, videos, magazines, celebrities, family, friends, and culture. Voices everywhere try to convince you of who you are, who you should be, how you should act, look, sound, dress, and more. It can be downright confusing. I might even call it an identity crisis.

So who are you?

If you're a follower of Jesus Christ, then your identity is in him! When Jesus died for our sins, he gave us the right to be called God's child (John 1:12). Before you are a daughter, a friend, a student, a girlfriend, a profile online, or anyone else, you are a child of God. You belong to him, and only his opinion matters. It's not a question of *who* you are but *whose* you are.

Over the next six weeks, we will learn truths from the Bible about who you are in Christ and what it means to be a child of God. I will show you Scripture about your identity, tell you stories, ask you questions, and challenge you to study the Bible so that you remember who God says you are. Grab a pen and a notebook to answer questions each day and write down what God is teaching you about your identity in Christ.

As you travel through life, I pray you'll carry these truths as if you stuffed them in a suitcase, unpacking them whenever you need them and sharing them with others you meet on your way. When the world tries to tell you who you should be, remember, you are a child of God.

God bless you!

Hannah

*"May the L*ORD* bless you and protect you; may the L*ORD* make his face shine on you and be gracious to you; may the L*ORD* look with favor on you and give you peace." Numbers 6:24–26*

Week 1

"Remember what happened
long ago, for I am God, and
there is no other; I am God,
and no one is like me."
Isaiah 46:9

Made in God's Image

*So God created man in his own image; he created him in
the image of God; he created them male and female.*
Genesis 1:27

I was obsessed with horses as a child. I would hover over blank sheets of paper for hours, attempting to create the exact image of a horse. First, I used tracing paper to really get the details down. Eyes squinted and teeth clamped, I got close. Yet my attempts were amateur. The drawings were never *exact* images. They could not be.

Did you know that you and I were not only created by God, but we also were created in the *image* of God? The teachers of the early church called this the *imago dei*, or the image of God. He is the artist, and he is no elementary school-aged amateur scribbling, tracing, and struggling to get the details right.

Did you know there is not a person on this planet you have met who is not made in God's image? Read that sentence again.

Christians have worked for centuries to determine what it means to be made in God's image. Book after book has been written on the subject. You may think it is about how we look, but it is more about our souls than our physical bodies. God is the creator, and he gave us the ability to create. God exists in the perfect community of the Father, Son, and Holy Spirit (the Trinity), and he created us to be in community with

one another. God brought order into the world, and he helps us bring order into our lives. We are all like little reflections of God.

Being created in God's image can remind you of your value and of the value of others. Everyone in this world is made in God's image, so everyone in the world has inherent dignity and is worthy of respect and honor. Even our enemies (or frenemies) are made in God's image and deserve our respect, honor, love, and kindness. It might seem impossible to be kind to someone who is unkind to us or who makes us mad, but all things are possible with God. He can help you love even the most unloving person.

So whether you are making a video, drawing something awesome for a school project, or writing in your notebook, smile a little bigger today.

Remember, you are made in the image of God, and so is everyone around you!

In Case You Want to . . .

Reflect

1. Who do you struggle to believe is made in God's image? Pray that God would change your heart.

2. Everyone is made in the image of God. How does knowing that affect the way you treat others? How does it change the way you treat yourself?

Take a moment to thank God for making you in his image. This is such an honor! Ask him to help you see other people as made in God's image too. If there is someone you are struggling to respect or be kind to, ask God to help you see them the way he does.

Keep Reading

Read Colossians 3:1–10. We reflect God's image, but only one person showed (and shows) God's image perfectly—Jesus. For those who are in Christ or following Jesus, what are we supposed to "put to death" or stop doing? (Hint: read verses 5–9.) What are we supposed to "put on"? Whose image do we reflect? (Read verse 10.)

Forgiven

*"I am the one, I sweep away your transgressions for
my own sake and remember your sins no more."*
Isaiah 43:25

I spent my wedding day avoiding food because it might stain my beautiful dress. I was slightly paranoid. Why? Because stains on white are impossible to remove, and I am a magnet for messes. There I sat in my beautiful, sparkling-white wedding dress, stomach grumbling as I stared at the food. Someone slid a plate in front of me. My mouth watered. Did I dare? *One bite.* The food was BBQ, meatballs, and mushrooms. If I dropped one bite, it would stain my dress forever! Maybe there was some sort of bib I could wear that would cover my entire dress? Short of using a tablecloth, I was out of luck.

I watched my husband eat, my bridesmaids eat, the groomsmen chow down, and all the guests eat, smiles on their faces. *Yes, I had to have one bite.* With surgeon-like precision, I cut my food and took micro-nibbles!

Sin, or doing things our way instead of God's, is like a heavy stain on a white wedding dress. Unlike my dress obsession on my wedding day though, we can do nothing to avoid sin. We are all born with its stain on our hearts. We can scrub with all the best cleaners, but the stain is still

there. Nothing we try can remove our sin. Worst of all, our sin separates us from God.

Psalm 51:7 says, "Wash me, and I will be whiter than snow." The psalmist is asking God to wash away his sins. We need someone who can remove our sins for us. Isaiah, a prophet who lived before Jesus, wrote our sins are "transgressions." That means they are crimes, offenses, or felonies. Sin is a *big* deal. But God says he will sweep our crime away and remember our sins no more! He removes our sin-stain permanently.

One of Jesus's followers said in 1 John 1:9, "If we confess our sins, he [God] is faithful and righteous to forgive us our sins and to cleanse us from all unrighteousness." Jesus's sacrifice makes forgiveness of our sin-stain possible. We confess, or admit, we are wrong and need God's help and believe that Jesus's sacrifice is enough to save us. In return, he removes our sin-stain. He takes it away.

You may be aware of your transgressions. You may think you are so stained by sin that you can never be clean. That is a lie. The truth is there is no stain too messy for Jesus. God's forgiveness is greater than our biggest crime. We are forgiven. Forgiven! Our sins have been washed and scrubbed away, removed. No trace of them remains any-more. It is like we are whiter than my wedding dress—no stains at all!

Remember, when God sees us, he sees the perfection of his Son, Jesus.

In Case You Want to . . .

Reflect

1. In your own words, explain how sin is like a stain.

2. In your own words, how does God get rid of our sin-stain?

3. Why is it important for us to ask Jesus to remove our stain of sin?

When God scrubs away sin's stain, it is gone forever! If you are a child of God and have decided to follow Jesus, thank God for removing the stain of sin from your life. Ask him to show you how you can share this good news with others!

Keep Reading

Read Psalm 103:8–13. Your version of the Bible may use the phrase "fear God." The word *fear* means respect. It also means regarding someone highly enough that you follow them and what they say. Knowing this, what do you think it means that God has compassion on those who fear him?

Pursued

*"For the Son of Man [Jesus] has come
to seek and to save the lost."*
Luke 19:10

The mission was simple—find the golden pumpkin. My church planned a free, interactive, city-wide scavenger hunt for our community. Teams of families, friends, and coworkers wore matching shirts and made up funny team names. They knew their objective and were ready to win the coveted prize: a golden (spray-painted) pumpkin and gift cards!

As they searched for the pumpkin, each team carefully followed their leader's instructions. After teams completed tasks, their leaders sent new clues and challenges. For over an hour, the teams relentlessly pursued that pumpkin. They met many obstacles along the way: stoplights, traffic jams, and road construction were enough to test their will and even their faith that they would find it. Still, they kept going.

You and I are like the golden pumpkin. We are pursued. Not by teams of focused scavenger hunters—we are of far greater value than a spray-painted pumpkin. We are pursued by God!

In fact, God has been pursuing us since sin separated us from him in the garden of Eden. God sent Jesus to earth to "seek and save the lost." He wants everyone to know him (2 Peter 3:9).

Jesus went to great lengths to seek us. There is a famous story in Luke 15 called the parable of the lost sheep. Jesus told about a shepherd with one hundred sheep, but one was missing. That sheep would not survive long on its own. It needed to be rescued before it died or was killed by a predator.

So the shepherd left the other sheep that were together and safe, trudged into a dangerous wilderness, put himself in harm's way, and searched until he found the lost one. It was like an ancient scavenger hunt.

Jesus is like that good shepherd, but better. He is the God who will not stop searching for his people. It does not matter how long it takes; God cares for us too much to ever leave even one of us out on our own. Once we are found, we get to follow him, pursuing him too. Every time we talk to God, study the Bible, memorize Scripture, serve others in his name, and worship with other believers, we pursue God. And as we seek, or pursue, God, he makes us more like him (2 Corinthians 3:18). Our search for a golden pumpkin was nothing compared to Jesus's pursuit of one of his children.

Remember, God is pursuing us, and we can follow him in return.

In Case You Want to . . .

Reflect

1. What do you think it means to "pursue God"?

2. How are you pursuing God in your life now? What are some ways you can search for him with enthusiasm and faithfulness?

3. What changes do you believe God is asking you to make so that you can be more like him?

Thank God for making you more like his Son. Ask God to keep changing you as you pursue Jesus.

Keep Reading

Read Ephesians 2:1–10. Paul, who was a missionary and encourager of Christians after Jesus ascended to heaven, is writing to his friends in Ephesus (modern-day Turkey). What does Paul tell the Ephesians God has done for them? (You might have more than one answer to this question, and that is great!)

A Coheir

And if children, also heirs——heirs of God and
coheirs with Christ——if indeed we suffer with him
so that we may also be glorified with him.
Romans 8:17

It is through stories that deep truths are told. Things in life that are hard to explain can be better understood through word pictures that engage the imagination.

So here is a story for you that tells a very deep truth. It might sound familiar. There once was a girl who, though gentle and kind with many talents, never knew her identity. She did not know where she came from or where she was going. No one told her. She always felt like her life was missing something, but she could not figure it out. One day, a limousine pulled into her driveway and some official-looking men in suits knocked at her door.

"We're here for the daughter of the King," one man said.

The girl squinted, crinkling her nose, as she tried to make sense of the situation. "You must have the wrong address."

"No, miss," said the youngest man. "*You* are the daughter of the King."

If you have decided to follow Jesus, then you are a daughter of the King—God. And you, too, are an heir to the throne. You are an heiress.

When Jesus died on the cross for us, he made us coheirs—we inherit his inheritance! I have an adopted daughter who will receive the same inheritance as my biological children. We, too, inherit everything God has to offer because of Jesus.

Great! Where is the limo? Romans 8:17 reminds us that something else must come first. Since we will inherit what Jesus inherits, there will be times we suffer like he did. In Romans 8:18–24, God says we will have hardships in this life, but we are not alone, and one day, it will all be over. Everything will be glorious.

This may seem like a fictional fantasy, but it is not.

Remember, one day you will receive an inheritance because you are a daughter of the King.

In Case You Want to . . .

Reflect

1. Did you know Christians inherit whatever Jesus inherits? How does that make you feel?

2. What struggles are you facing?

3. Imagine an attorney called next week and said you were about to be given an inheritance. What would you hope to inherit—money? A mansion? How do those earthly things compare to the inheritance you will receive from God one day?

Take a moment and imagine all the things you will inherit from God one day. Get creative! Write your thoughts down. Pray, thanking him that one day all things will be made right, and the struggles will be worth it.

Keep Reading

Read Ephesians 3:1–13. Paul talks about a mystery that has not been made known to other generations until now. What is that mystery? (Hint: read verse 6.) How do you think Paul feels about this mystery of being a coheir? What questions do you have about being a coheir? Take your questions to a pastor or mentor.

Ruler

You made them a kingdom and priests to our
God, and they will reign on the earth.
Revelation 5:10

I grinned at the small plastic card In my hand. Finally, my driver's license! No more asking for rides, a little more independence, and now my older friends will take me seriously.

I was ready to rule the road!

I bounced to my car and plopped down in the driver's seat. Suddenly, my excitement waned. Wait. The gravity of what was happening fell on my shoulders. *How does turning sixteen make me capable of this? I am not a great driver. What if I crash? What if I hurt someone? I do not deserve to do this.*

In a way, I was *ruling* my part of the road. I had been given the responsibility and authority to drive. In the garden of Eden, God tasked Adam and Eve with ruling the earth and everything in it. That responsibility did not go away after they sinned. God makes us responsible to rule, reign, and care for things in our lives, big and small.

The Bible also says God's followers become coheirs of his kingdom with Jesus (Romans 8:17). They will rule for eternity. Jesus modeled how to rule in the way he sacrificially loved us and the way he cared for those in need. His rulership points us to God.

One day, God will put sin and death to death and create a new heaven and new earth. Our sin will be gone, and we will reflect Jesus even more than we do now. Instead of getting keys to a car, we get the keys to God's kingdom, and God will ask us to rule parts of that kingdom in a bigger and better way than we do now!

Talk about responsibility!

After that first day of driving, I sat in my little white car taking deep breaths. God *had* made me a ruler at that moment. Our responsibilities, whether they are having a driver's license or taking care of our rooms, our money, or our time, all point to greater responsibility. Let's reign and rule well here on earth so that we are ready for our positions in eternity.

Remember, God made you a ruler, and he gave you the best example: his Son.

In Case You Want to . . .

Reflect

1. How does it make you feel to know that one day, followers of Jesus will rule in eternity?

2. How can you reflect Jesus in the way you rule and reign in your life now?

3. Where are you "ruling" now? Are you ruling well? Explain.

Ask God to help you rule and reign in the areas of life he has put you in. He will help you! Thank him for allowing you to rule in heaven one day. That is so cool of him!

Keep Reading

Read Proverbs 4:5–27. What does wisdom have to do with being a ruler? Highlight any verses that stick out.

Filled with Power

For God has not given us a spirit of fear, but one of power, love, and sound judgment.
2 Timothy 1:7

Missed again. I did not even hit the bottom of the net this time. I groaned and chased the basketball.

"That's okay," Dad said. "Try again."

No matter how hard I tried, I could not make the shot. I was too short. Too little. Too weak. At least I was determined. My pigtails flopped over my shoulder as I ran, bare feet pounding the dusty ground. Dad set the goal by our gravel drive years before, and we would play for hours. He taught my brother and me to dribble on a dirt court, along with how to pivot, throw an elbow, pick and roll, and shoot. I had nailed most of the lessons, except shooting. But this day would be different.

I snatched up the ball, dribbled back to the goal, and grinned at Dad. He knelt. His hands gripped my waist and lifted me higher and higher. I focused on the rim until I dunked that ball. Swish! Nothing but net.

"Again," I cheered. He lifted me again and again.

I was little. I was weak. My dad was strong. He gave me the power to dunk that ball.

The Christian life is hard, but God fills his followers with power so that we can look more like his Son, Jesus. Paul reminds Timothy of

this while Paul was imprisoned in Rome. He was tired and preparing to face death. Most of his friends had abandoned him because many were embarrassed by the good news of Jesus. Paul tells Timothy to never be ashamed to tell others about God and to be ready to suffer for the sake of the good news of Jesus (2 Timothy 2:8). Timothy, like Paul, could not do it alone. God would have to empower him.

Following Jesus cost Paul everything, including his life. Though following Jesus today might not cost us our lives, hardship and sacrifice will come. Struggles are not a sign God has disappeared. Most often, in those challenging times, we feel his presence even more.

The cost of following Jesus will always be worth it (Luke 14:27–30). We cannot do it on our own, just as I could not make the shot on my own.

Remember, when we decide to follow Jesus, God fills us with his power to "make the shot," or live for him, because we cannot do it on our own.

In Case You Want to . . .

Reflect

1. Think of a time when you could not do something on your own and needed help. Explain.

2. In your own words, explain how God helps his followers live out their faith in him.

3. If you are a child of God, how is he helping you live out your faith?

If you follow Jesus, thank him for helping you live out your faith, even when life gets difficult. Ask him to empower you to live your life for him.

Keep Reading

Read Philippians 2:12–18. In verse 12 he tells the Philippian Christians to work out their salvation with fear and trembling. This does not mean we should be scared. We should respect God so much that we *want* to obey. We are not working *for* our salvation—we are working it out or living it out by doing what God asks of us. Knowing these things, who is working in us and helping us? How does this remind us we are being filled with his power?

7

Valuable

"So don't be afraid; you are worth more than many sparrows."
Matthew 10:31

Abby was amazing, which was why, as one of her teachers, I was perplexed when her parents requested a meeting. Their child was excelling in my class—she made perfect scores on all my tests except one, and that one was 98 percent. The meeting was a few days away, but I could sense her anxiety. One afternoon, I got called to the counselor's office, and there Abby sat, tears flowing. She poured out her heart, sharing her battle with depression and anxiety. My heart broke.

"Who am I if I don't get all 100s in every class?" She sobbed into her hands. "I have to be perfect."

My heart broke more.

There is constant pressure for everyone—especially teenagers—to produce value. You must get the highest grades, be a star athlete, land the lead in the play, or have the most curated social media to prove your worth to others. Even when other people are not asking us for perfection, we ask it of ourselves.

In Matthew 10, Jesus sends his disciples out to tell people about him. He tells them some people will not want to hear, and some people might want to harm them for being Christians. (This is called persecution.) They will expect the disciples to stop making such a fuss. That is

when Jesus tells his disciples that if he takes care of a small bird, then how much more valuable are they?

We are not valuable because of our accomplishments, good grades, skills, abilities, or what anyone else thinks. We are valuable because God says so. He loves us so much that he knows how many hairs we have on our heads (Matthew 10:30), and he knows our thoughts (Psalm 139:2)! We are so valuable that while we were still sinners, God sent his one and only Son to take the punishment for our sins so that anyone who believes in Jesus can have eternal life (Romans 5:8; John 3:16). Now that is value.

There is no grade Abby could have gotten that would make her any more valuable to God than she already was (and is). The disciples were not popular or valuable according to the world's standards. They were so disliked, in fact, that they were persecuted. But when the world did not care about them, God did.

Remember, God values his people because we are his!

In Case You Want to . . .

Reflect

1. Do you place your value in things you do or accomplish? Explain.

2. In your own words, write out how valuable you are to God.

3. Write down John 3:16, but put your name where it says, "the world."

You are so valuable. Ask God to help you understand your value. Thank him for loving you so much. If you do not feel how much God values you, remember, God's truths trump our feelings. Ask God to help you believe his truths even when you do not feel them.

Keep Reading

Read Romans 8:31–39. Look at verse 32 a little closer. Who did God give up so that we could be with him? How does this demonstrate how valuable we are to him? Read verses 35, 37–39 again. No one can separate us from God! How does this truth show our value to him?

Week 2

I will remember the LORD's works; yes, I will remember your ancient wonders.
Psalm 77:11

Adopted

He [God] predestined us to be adopted as sons through Jesus
Christ for himself, according to the good pleasure of his will.
Ephesians 1:5

Let me take you back in history . . . to the '80s. The era of neon cloth-ing, valley girls, big hair, and the craze of the Cabbage Patch doll. People lost their minds trying to buy this doll, and I had one. Blue eyes like mine, yellow yarn hair—*not* like mine—a plastic face and cotton-stuffed body—also *not* like mine. We did not simply "buy" her. We "adopted" her, and I had the certificate to prove it.

The Cabbage Patch doll marketers knew what they were doing. They wanted me to feel like my doll was part of my family. The value of a stable family environment is crucial in a child's development. A loving family promotes self-confidence and social and cognitive development in a child. Something tugs inside us to provide a home for those who need one.

I loved that my doll was adopted, but I could not grasp the full con-cept of *adoption* as a young girl. It was a make-believe game I thought I outgrew. But when I became a mom and adopted a daughter of my own, I understood the magnitude of this word. Adoption is forever-binding, the real deal, and a lifetime commitment.

Once adopted, a person becomes part of a family—a connection surpassing blood or biology. My adopted daughter is just as much mine as the daughter I gave birth to. She is entitled to any benefits of being part of our family or any inheritance given. It is as if she were born of me.

If we have faith in Jesus, you and I have been adopted into God's family. When God adopts us, we are bound to him and his family.

God wants to be our Father. Ephesians 1:5 tells us God decided long ago to adopt us into his family because it brings *him* great happiness! Me being a part of his family makes God happy!

God wants to adopt you. There is an open invitation to be adopted by him, to be a part of his family. Inviting you into his family makes him far happier than a giddy little '80s girl with her own Cabbage Patch doll. It even makes him happier than I was on the day my daughter became my own.

Remember, God delights in your adoption.

In Case You Want to . . .

Reflect

1. What is your "adoption story"—the story of how you first became a part of God's family?

2. Have you ever considered your adoption into God's family? How does that make you feel?

3. What are some benefits of being in God's family?

Thank God for wanting to adopt you and be your perfect father. If it is difficult to think of him as your father, that is okay. Ask him to help you see him that way.

Keep Reading

Read Galatians 4:1–7. Highlight verses 6 and 7. Though these verses say "son" or "sons," they mean sons and daughters. Who does verse 7 say God has made his sons and daughters? What does this passage teach you about being adopted into God's family?

Eternally Royal

You are a chosen race, a royal priesthood, a holy nation, a people for his [God's] possession, so that you may proclaim the praises of the one who called you out of darkness into his marvelous light.

1 Peter 2:9

The crown was heavier than I thought it would be. Not that I imagined I would ever hold it, let alone wear it. I stood at the center of the gym floor, a high school sophomore crowned homecoming queen.

There must be a mistake. Sophomores cannot be homecoming queens. *Right?*

The crowd in the stands cheered, and, while I was excited, I was afraid. I scanned the homecoming court to my right and left. Their shock mirrored my own. Eyes wide, mouths open, jaws slack—I understood their disbelief. The seniors appeared even more surprised. They stared at me, and I stared back. I scrunched my nose and winced. I felt sure I should apologize.

Flowers were plopped into my arms. The homecoming king— a senior—stood next to me. *Have the ballots been counted wrong?* I asked the principal if he was sure the results were right. He nodded and ushered me forward before I could protest further. *Maybe this is a dream.* I bit my lip until it hurt. *Nope, not a dream.* At a moment's notice, I had somehow become unexpected and undeserving royalty.

Because of Christ, we are royally. It is part of our identity, but it is way better than being crowned homecoming queen. In 1 Peter 2:9 the author reminds us we are "a chosen race, a royal priesthood, a holy nation, a people for his [God's] possession." Because Jesus paid for our sins, we are adopted into God's family. We are part of the royal family and free to choose to follow Jesus instead of sin!

I wore my crown for one night. Honestly, where else would I wear the colossal contraption? My reign lasted only a year, and the crown now resides on my memorabilia shelf. It is tarnished, faded, and missing several jewels.

Our royal reign as children of God is eternal. Our crowns do not fade, tarnish, or break. The jewels remain intact. Because of Jesus, we can walk taller, smile brighter, and on bad days, straighten our crowns.

Remember, we are eternally royal.

In Case You Want to . . .

Reflect

1. Do you see yourself as royal? Why or why not?

2. Read 1 Peter 2:11–17. How does or should your status in Jesus change the way you interact with other people?

3. How does being royal affect your life—how you live, treat your body, and treat other people?

Thank God for his generosity. If you are his child, then you are royal. That is such a generous gift! Ask him to help you use your royal status in a way that honors him in all you do and in all your interactions with others.

Keep Reading

Read Psalm 8:3–9. How does this passage remind you of being eternally royal?

Belong

If we live, we live for the Lord; and if we die, we die for the Lord. Therefore, whether we live or die, we belong to the Lord.
Romans 14:8

The year I moved schools, first-day jitters knotted my stomach. For weeks during the summer, I tossed and turned at night. Once, I dreamed of walking into my new school and no one talking to me. I had no friends. I did not fit in. I did not belong. What if that *actually* happened?

When the first day of school came, I stood near the doorway of my new class, listening to all the kids chattering. I missed my friends—leaving them behind felt like a big deal. I inched inside the room, first tucking my hands in my pockets then holding them at my side. I felt awkward. Everyone knew each other. They smiled, laughed, hugged, and joked. I was the outsider, and it felt lonely.

Everyone wants to fit in. We are hardwired to belong. When we feel like we do not belong, we may do everything in our power to change that—hanging with bad crowds or trying to impress the wrong people.

Romans 8:14 reminds us that followers of Jesus belong in God's family. We are his even when we do not belong in the world. We do not always need to know *where* we belong when we know *who* we belong to. Paul says whatever we do in this life or the next, we belong to the

Lord. We are reminded that we "fit in" when we follow God with our lives.

We remember we belong to him when we communicate with him by reading our Bibles and praying. We are reminded that we belong to him when we connect with a local church and other believers. We feel more like we belong to him as we serve people around us with our time, talents, and resources, and live out our faith with our words and actions.

I stood in the classroom doorway that first day feeling like an outsider. Then a girl I recognized approached me. We went to church together! In no time at all, I felt more at home in my new school than I had in my old school. One little reminder helped me remember who I belonged to: God.

We may never feel like we belong or fit in here, and that is okay. This world is not our forever home. For followers of Jesus, God's kingdom is our home.

Remember, God is who we belong with.

In Case You Want to . . .

Reflect

1. Describe a time when you felt out of place.

2. Where do you feel like you belong? Is it in a place or with certain people?

3. How does knowing God's children belong to him change your life?

God's family is filled with many kinds of people from all over the world! Even though we have differences, we all belong together and with God. Thank God for welcoming all kinds of people into his family, and thank him that you belong to him.

Keep Reading

Read Psalm 100:1–5. Think about it. How do these verses remind you that God's children belong to him? How does the writer of this psalm respond to this good news? How should all God's children react to knowing we belong to him?

Rewarded

*"But love your enemies, do what is good, and lend,
expecting nothing in return. Then your reward will
be great, and you will be children of the Most High.
For he is gracious to the ungrateful and evil."*
Luke 6:35

Did she just say reading books and pizza in the same sentence?! *Um, yes, please.*

To encourage students to read more, the "Book It!" program rewarded those who met their monthly reading goals with a gift certificate for a personal pizza from a local restaurant. Our family did not go out to eat a lot. Driving into town was a once-a-week excursion, and eating out was magical. Now I could get my own free pizza each month simply for reading? *When could I start?*

Each time I read a book, my teacher gave me the most beautiful sparkling star sticker to track the number of books I had read. After many books, the moment came: she walked toward me with a pizza gift certificate in hand—my reward! I earned it.

God's children are rewarded for the good works they do too. Our good works do not save us—that's Jesus's sacrifice for our sins—but Jesus did the best work for us. Because of him, we should also want to do good works for others.

In Luke 6:35, Jesus teaches his disciples how to follow him and what living out their faith should look like. Like my teacher gave me an incentive to read books, Jesus gave his followers an incentive: "Love your enemies, do what is good, lend, and expect nothing in return. Then your reward will be great."

Jesus asks his followers to represent him well. Sometimes we are rewarded for that during this lifetime, even if it is just the joy of knowing we represented Jesus well. But the Bible makes it clear we also have rewards waiting for us in eternity.

Jesus says in Revelation 22:12, "Look, I am coming soon, and my reward is with me to repay each person according to his work." He gives a reward to each person according to what they have done.

But what is the reward?

Paul quotes Isaiah 52 and 64, "What no eye has seen, no ear has heard, and no human heart has conceived—God has prepared these things for those who love him." We can only imagine the goodness that is in store for us.

Remember, when our love for God spills over into our love for other people, we will be rewarded.

In Case You Want to . . .

Reflect

1. Think of a time when you were rewarded for something good you did. How did it make you feel?

2. How does knowing God rewards his followers for the way they represent him make you want to live your life?

3. What rewards from God do you see in your life now?

Ask God to examine your heart and your life. Ask him to show you ways you can continue to serve him or new ways he wants you to serve him. Thank him for the rewards he has given you now and for the ones to come!

Keep Reading

Read Colossians 3:23–24. What does this passage tell you about being rewarded?

On His Mind

God, how precious your thoughts are to me; how vast their sum is! If I counted them, they would outnumber the grains of sand; when I wake up, I am still with you.
Psalm 139:17–18

We would rather not talk about *that* year. In fact, if I could erase it altogether, I would. The year 2020 was terrible. My family lost ten loved ones, including my granny. Months after Granny passed, my husband's grandma, a mother figure in his life, died unexpectedly as well. It was *hard.*

For months, my family juggled mounds of grief alongside the isolation of a pandemic. Still, friends and family cared for and surrounded me from a distance like never before. I received countless cards saying, "Thinking of you!" and "We're praying for you and your family." Many brought meals or sent flowers to show their love and support.

God showed his love for us through the love of our community. He considered us precious enough to love, value, and hold during a rough patch. God's mind is on his children!

Like we think about the ones we love, God's thoughts are on us. Psalm 139:17–18 says God's thoughts about us are precious and many, so many that they outnumber the grains of sand!

God thinks about us because he loves us. His love is too big to be fully explained or understood. Ephesians 3:18–19 tells us God's love for us is deep, wide, and high, and it surpasses knowledge! It is as if he is smiling wide, considering how much he loves us, and all the ways he will show us his care.

Here are a few ways we can see his love: he provides people to love and support us (Galatians 6:2), he causes everything to work together for the good (Romans 8:28), and every good gift he gives us in our lives is from God and for our enjoyment (James 1:17). The God of all creation has you on his mind!

Remember, you are his precious daughter. His thoughts about you cannot be counted!

In Case You Want to . . .

Reflect

1. Who is on your mind more than anyone else? How do you show love to that person?

2. Think of a time when you felt loved by someone. How did they show you were on their mind?

3. How has God shown you he is thinking about you this week?

Write out your good thoughts about God. If there are any "bad" thoughts or questions you have for him, write those down too. God can handle anything you bring to him. He loves you, and he cares about your questions.

Keep Reading

Read Psalm 40:1–5. King David, a great king of Israel, wrote many of the psalms, which are songs or poems to God. What were some of David's thoughts about God? What did God do for him? What does this teach you about God?

Free

For freedom, Christ set us free. Stand firm, then,
and don't submit again to a yoke of slavery.
Galatians 5:1

People either love or hate escape rooms. On this day, I hated them. How did I end up here? One of my wrists was tied to an iron pipe mounted on a wall in a small room. At least I was not alone, though the others were no help. Not even my husband!

I sighed and jiggled my hand but could not free myself. I scanned the room, a prisoner to the iron pipe, while a large timer on the wall counted down. There had to be a way out of these shackles. A bookcase stood to my right and a small table was beneath the pipe. I searched the table. A key! I willed my fingers to stretch further until they grabbed the key . . . but it slipped, falling in slow motion to the ground just out of my reach. Just then, out of the corner of my eye, I saw my husband walking over. He picked up the key, and I was free.

I left the handcuff and did not look back. *Time to help everyone else escape the room!*

All followers of Jesus have been set free! No longer are we hand-cuffed to sin, unable to release ourselves from its grip. Jesus held the key, and he released us. Galatians 5:1 says Jesus set us free so that we could be free—not so that we could return to being in bondage.

The churches in Galatia (modern-day Turkey) had a problem. In this region, some Jewish people had become followers of Jesus. Many non-Jewish people, or Gentiles, followed Jesus too. Some Jewish Christians were teaching that all Christians had to trust Jesus to forgive sin *and* follow the Old Testament law in order to be saved. Confusion grew between the two groups of believers. Did they or did they not have to trust Jesus *and* perfectly obey the law?

Paul settled their debate. He told the Galatians Jesus had set them free from sin. Though the law is good for helping us make wise choices, it cannot save us. It never could. God gave the law to show we can never live up to his standards. We cannot free ourselves no matter how hard we try. Only Jesus can rescue us.

Sometimes we try to please God by following rules. We think he will love us more if we look like the best Christian or avoid the "worst" sins. The truth is, nothing can save us any more than Jesus already did.

We were once bound to the law, held captive by sin and its punishment—separation from God. Paul argues Jesus's sacrifice alone frees us from sin. When we try to please God with rule-following, we are reaching for the wrong key. It is not Jesus *and* the law. It is just Jesus. We are no longer cuffed to sin like I was cuffed to that iron pipe in an escape room.

Remember, Jesus is our key, and we are free!

In Case You Want to . . .

Reflect

1. Why do you think it is impossible for us to follow all of God's laws?

2. Why did we need someone to free us from the law?

3. Who freed us, and why do you think that is good news?

God has set his children free from the law we could not keep on our own. If you are a child of God, celebrate this good news! Thank God for sending his Son, Jesus, to set us free. Ask him to give you opportunities to share this good news with others so they can be free too!

Keep Reading

Read Romans 6:6–11. God has set us free from sin and its punishment. We no longer live under the old law. Romans 6:6–11 shares we have been set free from something else too. What is it? How does knowing this affect your life?

Prayed For

"I pray not only for these, but also for those who believe in me through their word. May they all be one, as you, Father, are in me and I am in you. May they also be in us, so that the world may believe you sent me."
John 17:20–21

It was too late to be awake, but I could not sleep. I lay on my side, a pillow between my knees. Sleeping comfortably as a pregnant mom with a military husband deployed overseas is not an easy task. That night, I felt a strong nudge to pray for my husband, Stephen. I could not shake him from my mind. I grabbed my journal from the nightstand and began to write out a prayer for him.

Several weeks passed with no word from Stephen. As the days dragged on, I prayed any time I thought of him. After a month without a word, he finally called. *Sweet relief.*

He apologized and explained the battles had been intense. During one battle, he fell into the street and had to keep still as bullets whizzed around him. Some people in his unit died, but he was never hit. Chill bumps covered my body when I realized this battle happened the same night I was unable to sleep—the night I felt prompted to pray. Even thousands of miles apart, God connected us through prayer.

On the night Jesus was betrayed and arrested, he was praying.

When Jesus says in John 17, "but also for those who believe in me through their word," he refers to future believers. He prayed that they "all be one, as you, Father, are in me and I am in you . . . so that the world may believe you sent me." This prayer is called the high priestly prayer. Our unity, or oneness, causes others to believe in Jesus! Jesus brought unity between me and my husband that night through prayer, but you do not have to be married to experience oneness with other Christians.

We are unified when we follow Jesus by studying the Bible together and praying for each other; when we choose not to gossip about one another; and when we hold each other accountable to not fall into temptation. Jesus cares so much about our unity that he prays for it, and, whether on a battlefield or in your bedroom, he invites us to pray for it too.

When I prayed for my husband's safety and protection, Jesus had already prayed for oneness between us. Yes, because we are husband and wife, but also because we both follow Jesus.

Remember, it is Jesus's desire that you have unity with other Christians.

In Case You Want to . . .

Reflect

1. Read Romans 8:34. Did you know Jesus prayed for you and is still praying for you? How does this make you feel?

2. How does knowing Jesus himself is praying for you affect your life?

3. How is your prayer life going? Do you pray often, or do you need to pray more? Do you pray with friends? How could your prayer life be strengthened?

Thank God for the privilege of being able to talk to him any time through prayer. Thank him for praying for you! Ask God to strengthen your prayer life. He wants to hear from you and help you!

Keep Reading

Read 1 Thessalonians 5:12–20. What do these verses tell you about prayer? According to these verses, what is God's will for us? What does this teach you about the importance of prayer?

Week 3

"Be careful not to forget the LORD who brought you out of the land of Egypt, out of the place of slavery."
Deuteronomy 6:12

Planned

"For I know the plans I have for you"—this is the Lord's declaration—"plans for your well-being, not for disaster, to give you a future and a hope."
Jeremiah 29:11

Confession: I like planning so much that I have a five-year, color-coded agenda. I know, it's extra. I *enjoy* writing my plans—it makes me happy! When I get things done, life runs smoothly, and it is my way of showing the people in my life that I care about them. I am *not* a wing-it kind of gal. So when my planner went missing for almost forty-eight hours last year, I was distraught. Every important deadline I had was written there. Sweat beaded my forehead, and a big ball of panic formed in my stomach. I was forced to wing it. *Great.*

There is nothing "wing it" about God. He planned for us, and he has plans for us. God says in Jeremiah 29:11, "'For I know the plans I have for you'—this is the Lord's declaration—'plans for your well-being, not for disaster, to give you a future and a hope.'"

When Jeremiah wrote these words, God's people were in exile. They were far from home, and because of their sin, they felt even farther from God. Was God sticking to his plan? Had he not promised to bless them? They felt like God had thrown out his agenda on purpose and decided to "wing it" instead.

You may sometimes feel like God is "winging" your life. You might not be able to see the plans God has for you. It might feel like you are in exile, and you cannot see the end. You may have messed up big time. You may be winging your life without asking God for direction, like the Israelites did. But do not forget this: even though the Israelites messed up, and even in their worry, fear, and sin, God was in control. He is an expert planner!

Before time began, God set his plan in motion. Like the Israelites, your mistakes and burdens are no surprise to God. You are wanted, loved, cared for, and part of his plan. He prepared for you, and you are here at this moment, in this time in history on purpose.

Even during hardships, and even when it seems like God is not near, God's plans for your life are good. You can trust God's plan despite your circumstances. Cast your worries on him and trust his plans for you (1 Peter 5:7).

Whether you are a planner or a "wing it" gal, whether this season of your life is happy or hard, let God determine your steps.

Remember, his plans are best, and he is in control.

In Case You Want to . . .

Reflect

1. Are you a planner? Or do you like to wing it? How have you seen some of God's plans in your life already?

2. Have you ever felt like you were in exile? How does it make you feel to know that God was in control?

3. How does knowing God has a plan for you influence the way you live?

Thank God for making plans for your life. Ask him to help you make the right decisions on your journey through life.

Keep Reading

Read Matthew 6:25–34. What does Jesus tell us to do? (Hint: read verse 25.) Why do you think Jesus tells us not to worry? Who will take care of us? Whether you are a planner or not, ask yourself how you can better trust God in the good and challenging times.

Worth Saving

God's love was revealed among us in this way:
God sent his one and only Son into the world
so that we might live through him.
1 John 4:9

I choked on giggles as my six-year-old legs carried me through the field, faster and faster. I ran from my brother and darted to the crab apple tree. A rotten apple squished between my toes, shooting a sour stench right to my nose, but I kept running. Our game of chase morphed into dodging rotten crab apples. With each step, my feet mushed apples until I could no longer stand the smell or the sensation of apple goo caked on my feet. The rotten stench covered us, and it would take serious effort to get it off.

Long ago there was another fruit tree. When God created the world, he made a garden in Eden and placed this tree, among others, there. God said the world was good.

God made the first two people, Adam and Eve, and gave them everything they could want. They had countless fruit trees from which to eat except one—God told them not to eat the fruit from the tree in the middle of the garden. If they did, they would die. God's enemy, Satan, disguised as a snake, tricked them and whispered lies into their ears. They wouldn't *really* die. They could be *like* God. They disobeyed God and ate from the tree. Their choice brought sin into the world.

Sin cursed the earth and everyone in it. It separates us from God. It is like the crab apples I stepped on as a little girl—rotten, stinky, and sticky. I took a bath to remove the crab-apple goo, but no one can get rid of their sin. The payment for all sin is death (Romans 6:23).

When Adam and Eve sinned, God told them about the curse of sin. God also made a promise to Eve. One day, someone would come from her family and destroy God's enemy and the power of sin in this world. Just like everyone was cursed through Adam and Eve's sin, everyone would be blessed through the one God promised (Genesis 3:15).

Jesus is the promised one, and God kept his promise. God sent his Son to earth, making a way for you and me to be with him again forever. Jesus, God's Son, lived a perfect life and paid the price for our sin by dying in our place. Three days later, he defeated death by rising from the dead! Anyone who follows Jesus becomes a child of God (John 3:16). God loves you, and he says you're worth saving! While the payment for sin is death, the gift of God is eternal life (Romans 6:23). Where sin rots, Jesus restores!

Remember, even though this world is rotten with sin, God kept his promise to restore it. He sent his Son Jesus! He says you're worth saving!

In Case You Want to . . .

Reflect

1. What does sin do to your heart? Why do you think God hates sin?

2. Did you know God always planned to send his Son? How does it make you feel to know God made a way for you to be with him?

3. Is there anyone whom you're tempted to think isn't "worth saving"? Ask God to change your heart.

Thank God for what he did for you. If there's someone you know who doesn't yet follow Jesus, pray for them. Ask God to help them know how much he loves them.

Keep Reading

Read Genesis 3:13–15. Genesis 3:15 is considered the first prophecy of the gospel. (Theologians call this the *protevangelium*.) Read verse 15 again. How do these verses remind you that God keeps his promises?

A Disciple

"If anyone serves me, he must follow me. Where I am, there my servant also will be. If anyone serves me, the Father will honor him."
John 12:26

My palms were wet with sweat and my knuckles white as I held on to the steering wheel. Seventy miles per hour—that is how fast my heart raced. But the speedometer on my tiny white sedan read thirty miles per hour. How was I driving *below* the speed limit?

"You're doing great," Mom said. Moms have to say things like that, but I appreciated her encouragement. She patted my leg. "Just keep your eyes on the road."

Right. I gulped. *Eyes on the road. Stay focused.* Why was driving this difficult? I had read the driving manual multiple times and aced the permit test, but when it came to putting wheels on the road, I was terrified.

"Just keep your eyes on the road, sweetheart." Mom's simple, but vital, instruction has stayed with me all these years. I have found them to be a good standard for being a follower or disciple of Jesus too. *"Just keep your eyes on Jesus."*

In John 12:26, Jesus says to a crowd that if they want to serve him, they must follow him. When he said those words, Jesus had just entered Jerusalem for one purpose: to die for the sins of the world. When Jesus

said, "If anyone serves me, he must follow me," he was inviting us to something hard but good—to be his disciples.

A disciple is a learner or student. When we decide to follow Jesus, we become *his* student. We learn to be like him. But just like I could not learn to drive by only reading the driver's manual, we do not learn to be a disciple only by reading and knowing all the things. We learn when we begin to put our knowledge into practice. This means things like reading the Bible and doing what it says, serving others, worshiping with other followers, and encouraging one another to grow in our faith.

Being a disciple of Jesus might be difficult at times, and that is okay. You are not alone. If you are a disciple of Jesus, keep your eyes on the road.

Remember, when you look at him, you will learn how to navigate life as his disciple.

In Case You Want to . . .

Reflect

1. In your own words, explain what a disciple is.

2. What are disciples of Jesus supposed to do? List some ways you can follow him.

3. How does your life show you are a disciple or follower of Jesus? List two or three ways you are following him.

Following Jesus will not always be easy. If you are a child of God, he will help you follow him. Thank him for allowing you to be his disciple. Ask him to help you follow him every day.

Keep Reading

Read Matthew 4:18–22. In this passage, Jesus has started his ministry. What do these verses say about being a disciple of Jesus? Do the men go with him or stay behind? Do you think they were excited to follow Jesus? Why or why not?

Gifted

Just as each one has received a gift, use it to serve
others, as good stewards of the varied grace of God.
1 Peter 4:10

A red carpet, VIP, movie premiere event? I rubbed my eyes, staring at the email. *Is this spam?* Nope. Totally legit. I read it again just to make sure and laughed aloud. It said we would get to meet some of the actors too! *Squeal!* A movie company had somehow landed on my little website and asked me to review their movie in exchange for ten VIP movie premiere tickets. Ten tickets! Um, what an amazing gift was this? All I had to do was write a review and post it online? *Yep. This is happening.*

The ten tickets given to me were awesome, but sharing them was even more incredible. The best gifts are the ones we get to share with others.

Followers of Jesus have spiritual gifts we get to share with people. These are not character traits, natural skills, or talents (although those are given to us by God too). In 1 Corinthians 12, Paul lists many of these gifts, such as wisdom, faith, prophecy, and healing. Paul lists other spiritual gifts like teaching, service, mercy, and generosity in Romans 12. These gifts are freely given to us. We do not do anything to deserve them; God is simply kind to us. In his kindness, he asks us to use our gifts to "serve others."

Each follower of Jesus receives at least one spiritual gift (1 Corinthians 12:7), and no gift is more important than another (1 Corinthians 12:21–26). God also tells us to use our gifts to help others (1 Peter 4:10) and that using them deepens our relationships with God (Ephesians 4:13).

There are many spiritual gifts and many ways to use them. For example, the gift of encouragement might mean you can encourage others in their faith. If you have the gift of hospitality, you might use that gift to make someone feel welcome by inviting them to sit with you at school. Those who have the gift of service can help people who have physical needs. The possibilities for using our gifts are endless.

The best part of the VIP movie experience was sharing it with my friends!

Remember, if God is the giver of good gifts, we are the receivers. And the best gifts are the ones we get to share with others.

In Case You Want to . . .

Reflect

1. Do you know what your spiritual gifts are? (If you need help finding out what your spiritual gifts are, you can take a spiritual gifts assessment online or just start serving in your local church.)

2. List the gifts you believe God has given you.

3. Are you using those gifts to serve others? If so, how? If not, how might you be able to use your gifts?

Take a moment to thank God for giving good gifts. Ask him to show you what your gifts are if you are not sure. Ask him to help you know how and when to use the gifts he has given you.

Keep Reading

Read 1 Corinthians 13:1–13. Followers of God are all given different gifts to serve others, but if we do not love others, those gifts do not do any good. What does 1 Corinthians 13 teach you about love and using your spiritual gifts?

Known

*Lᴏʀᴅ, you have searched me and known me. You
know when I sit down and when I stand up; you
understand my thoughts from far away.*
Psalm 139:1–2

It took years, but my husband and I reached a mysterious new level in
our marriage: mind reading. (No, this is not sci-fi—you are still reading
the right book.) I had only heard of it from older couples. They would say,
"Wait and see. It will happen to you." *Weird.*

I did not even know it was happening at first. He would send me a
text at the same time I was thinking about him, or we would finish each
other's sentences. It kept evolving until we started saying the exact
same things! Now, on his way home from work, he sometimes stops
at a store and brings me my favorite candy bar or soda on a day I am
craving it!

My husband knows all my quirks, likes, and dislikes, and I know his.
I want to know him and be known by him. It feels good to be known,
but there was a time in my life I felt very unknown. In middle school, no
one understood me or knew the real me. I was not even sure how well I
knew myself! Even now, as well as my husband knows me, as well as I
think I know myself, God is the only one who fully knows me. God is the
only one who *fully* knows you, too, because he is the one who made you.

Psalm 139:1–2 says God searches us, deep inside, every square inch, and he knows us. He knows us so well that he understands our thoughts even from far away. The psalmist continues a few verses later, "Before a word is on my tongue, you know all about it, Lᴏʀᴅ" (Psalm 139:4). God knows not only what we are thinking but also what we will say before the words are even in our mouths. He knows it all—when we go to sleep, when we wake up, and even how many hairs are on our heads!

Being known gives us security and belonging. You may feel known by your best friend, your mom or dad, or a sibling.

You may also feel known by nobody at all, as I did in middle school. God gave you the desire to be known. It points us to God, the only one who can know us fully. It's like there is a God-shaped hole inside us that *only* he can fill, no matter how known or unknown you feel by people around you.

I am so glad to be known by my husband, but I am so glad to be known *so much more* by God. My love for my husband grows and deepens as I get to know him more, and my love for God grows and deepens as I get to know *him* more. When we grow in our relationships with God, we discover comfort, security, and belonging.

Remember, not even the most intuitive husband, the best friend, or the perfect parent knows you the way God does.

In Case You Want to . . .

Reflect

1. Who knows you best?

2. God knows you better than you know yourself. How does this truth affect your life?

God fully knows you! Thank him for knowing you so well. Go to him with all your wins, losses, heartaches, and worries. He cares for you.

Keep Reading

Read Psalm 139:7–18. According to these verses, how well does God know you? Highlight your evidence and explain how these verses reveal you are fully known by God.

Provided For

And my God will supply all your needs according
to his riches in glory in Christ Jesus.
Philippians 4:19

I am staring at my computer. Sometimes words do not flow freely. Other times they gush out of me like water from a firehose. The cursor blinks slowly like it is counting the seconds, but my mind is racing. I search my memories and experiences of how God has provided for me. It is not that I cannot think of one story—it is that there are too many.

For over thirty years now, I have followed God imperfectly, and he has taken care of me in ways I never expected. I see his provision in my life through family wounds healed, broken relationships restored, prayers answered, dollars stretched, money provided when finances were tight, friendships forged, and more. Even when some situations remained unresolved, he reminded me of his presence. When wounds were still raw, relationships were still broken, and when my questions felt unanswered—he was there.

Paul spent two years in prison after an angry mob wanted him dead. When he wrote Philippians 4:19, Paul was facing many trials and much suffering, yet he spoke of God's provision for him. Paul knew God provides for us even when our situations seem bleak. God knows what we need before we ask.

Paul was right. Jesus told his disciples, "Your Father knows the things you need before you ask him. . . . Don't worry, saying, 'What will we eat?' or 'What will we drink?' or 'What will we wear?'" (Matthew 6:8, 31–32). He reminded them their heavenly Father knew what they needed. God will provide for you when you feel lonely and in need of a friend. God will care for you when others might be talking bad about you. God sees you even if you feel invisible. He is telling you how much he loves you when you stare in the mirror feeling unlovable. He cares for you when your family might be falling apart.

Above everything we think we need—the perfect family, the nicest clothes, awesome friends—Jesus tells us to "seek first the kingdom of God and his righteousness" (Matthew 6:33). We are to make God the top priority. God provides for our need to know him through his Word, the Bible, communicating with him in prayer, and Christian community. Pursue him. Read his Word. Love him and love others.

God has provided for me in obvious and not-so-obvious ways. If you are following Jesus, I am praying you will count all the ways God provides for you.

Remember, when you look for him, you will see him everywhere, providing for you.

In Case You Want to . . .

Reflect

1. In your own words, write Philippians 4:19. What does this verse mean?

2. How have you seen God provide for others?

3. How have you seen him provide for you? List as many ways as you can think of.

God cares for every person in the world. He loves them so much, yet he takes exceptional care of his children. Whether you are a follower of Jesus or not, take a moment to recall specific ways only God could have provided for you. Thank him.

Keep Reading

Read Psalm 107:1–9. How do these verses remind you of God's provision? Explain.

Seen and Heard

The eyes of the L<small>ORD</small> are on the righteous, and
his ears are open to their cry for help.
Psalm 34:15

I forced myself up from my bed and pulled my prayer box from beneath the bed. My dad made the prayer box for me during my freshman year. It was wood and came with a slit on top and a lock. I decorated it to give it a little glam.

I knew God was prompting me to pray, but my head pounded, and my stomach cramped. I pressed my fingertips to my temples and rubbed, but the pain did not let up. Then the cramping started—*ugh*. I curled into a ball on my bed, held onto my pillow, and tried not to cry as the anxiety bubbled within me. My tears started to flow down my cheeks, all because of this period.

No amount of medicine helped, and I would often miss a day or two of school each month. It was terrible, especially since I was taking advanced classes. Missing any amount of time put me behind. I reached for a slip of paper, penned my prayer, and dropped it in the box, but I wondered if God *really* cared about my period pain. Every other girl has a period. It felt silly, like I was bothering God to go to him with this request.

Psalm 34:15 reminds me that God saw me and heard me. The "righteous" means those who are "right" with God. Followers of Jesus are only righteous because of what Jesus did for us. (We cannot follow God perfectly.) Also, notice the word LORD in this verse. When we see LORD spelled out like this, it indicates the author is using God's personal name. In this verse, the author reveals God himself sees and hears us. He *personally* comes close to us.

Philippians 4:6 says, "Don't worry about anything, but in everything, through prayer and petition with thanksgiving, present your requests to God." When we go to God in prayer, he not only sees us and hears us, but he also *keeps* our prayers. Revelation 5:8 says, "Each . . . had a harp and golden bowls filled with incense, which are the prayers of the saints." God values the prayers of his people. He loves them. He loves us!

Wherever we are, whatever we are going through—good, bad, or PMS—we can go to God with every burden. His eyes are on us, and his ears hear our cries.

Remember, he sees you and hears you.

In Case You Want to . . .

Reflect

1. Have you ever felt like no one could "see or hear" you? That no one understood what you were going through? Explain.

2. How does knowing that God sees and hears you address your life right now?

Whatever you are going through or whatever you will go through, God knows your worries more than you do. Thank him for listening, understanding, and caring for you. Remember to go to him with everything. He wants to hear from you!

Keep Reading

Read Psalm 18:1–17. Highlight how these verses relate to God hearing and seeing you. What does God do for those who cry out to him?

Week 4

*My soul, bless the
L*ORD*, and do not forget
all his benefits.
Psalm 103:2*

Liked

*For the L*ORD* takes pleasure in his people; he*
adorns the humble with salvation.
Psalm 149:4

Only *four* likes? Ugh. Do you know how much effort went into making that fifteen-second video of my adorable dogs? Of course you know! Or you can at least respect the time and effort I put into it. They were zooming across the yard in matching bandannas and spinning in circles like an adorable circus act. I even added circus music!

When I post on social media, I *know* it is not about the likes. My brain understands that my value is not found in how many shares or comments a post gets, but sometimes my heart forgets.

The internet is fun, and it helps us connect with people—but it is not real life. It is a highlight reel. Even when we post sad or vulnerable things, the truth is, we are showing only slices of our lives—not the whole picture. Even without social media, there's a pressure to be liked by the popular crowds or noticed by important people. In case you have forgotten, God's opinion of you (and what you post) is the only one that matters.

And guess what? God not only loves you, but he also *likes* you. Is there a difference?

Yep.

You can love your pet but not always like them. You can love your friends but not always like them. You can love your siblings but not always like them. You can even love your parents but not always like them. Our affection is limited. Our love and liking are not as intertwined as they should be. Our hearts are jealous, they hold grudges, and they are not thankful. That is why I am so glad God is different from us.

Read Psalm 149:4 again. The Lord takes pleasure in, or *delights* in, his people. He *likes* us and *loves* us on our most post-worthy days and on the days we want to hide from everyone.

If you are a follower of Jesus, part of your identity is being someone God delights in. You are liked by God, the creator of the universe and everything in it! Are you fangirling yet?

The number of likes you receive does not matter. Who likes you does not matter either.

Remember, you are liked by God, and his affection is the most important.

In Case You Want to . . .

Reflect

1. Do you worry about how many likes, shares, or comments you get when you post online? If you do not have social media, do you think those things would worry you?

2. How does it feel to know God delights in you?

3. How will knowing this fact help you navigate your feelings about social media, friends, and life?

Take a moment and put your name in Psalm 149:4. "For the LORD takes pleasure in his (your name); he adorns the humble with salvation." Thank God that you are liked and loved by him. Ask him to make you more like him every day.

Keep Reading

Read Zephaniah 3:9–20. In these verses, God is talking to his people in Israel. What does God do for his people that shows he delights in them? List at least three things you notice.

Filled with Fruit

But the fruit of the Spirit is love, joy, peace, patience, kindness, goodness, faithfulness, gentleness, and self-control. The law is not against such things.
Galatians 5:22–23

Imagine a tree that produces multiple kinds of fruit. Apples on one branch, pears on another, clusters of grapes, too, or maybe even strawberries and bananas! Those who follow Jesus are like this imaginary tree. The Holy Spirit fills us with all kinds of fruit, including love, joy, peace, patience, kindness, goodness, faithfulness, gentleness, and self-control.

Paul listed this fruit in the book of Galatians, a letter written to Christians living in Galatia. Before knowing Jesus, the Galatians had a different history from the Jewish people who worshiped God. Their culture was probably influenced by the Celts, a large group of fierce and respected warriors in ancient Europe. (Did I mention I am a former history teacher? I love this stuff.)

When the good news of Jesus was shared with the Galatians by Christians, Paul reminded them that once they were saved, their hearts were made new. Like a rotten tree produces bad fruit, a heart far away from Jesus produces sin. Galatians 5:19–21 says, "the works of the flesh are obvious: sexual immorality, moral impurity, promiscuity,

idolatry, sorcery, hatreds, strife, jealousy, outbursts of anger, selfish ambitions, dissensions, factions, envy, drunkenness, carousing, and anything similar." In Galatians 5, Paul reminded the Galatians that they didn't have to live in their "flesh" anymore! Because they were saved, their lives as followers of Jesus could be marked by "good fruit." People should see this fruit in the everyday lives of Christians.

No fruit stands on its own. Since Paul says "fruit" of the Spirit, not "fruits," he means that we can't have one without having the other. The Holy Spirit doesn't cultivate love without self-control, joy without peace, kindness without patience, or any one fruit without the other.

For Christians, the Holy Spirit is harvesting all the fruit in our hearts, and we can join him in that work by following God with our lives and doing things like studying the Bible and valuing what it says. We love other people with our words and actions; give our time, talents, and money back to God; worship God with other believers; share the gospel with friends and family; and pray to God.

By living out our faith and seeking God, the Holy Spirit grows fruit in our lives. Then we will be like the branches of an amazing tree—producing the fruit of the Spirit!

Remember, God's children are filled with beautiful fruit.

In Case You Want to . . .

Reflect

1. Write out the fruit of the Spirit.

2. Are you still living like you are in "the flesh"? How do you see God changing the fruit of your heart?

3. How has someone else's fruit helped you?

Ask God to develop the fruit of the Spirit in your life. If you are unable to see any fruit in your life, ask God why. Talk to a parent, pastor, or church leader about why you feel fruitless.

Keep Reading

Read James 2:14–26. James was Jesus's brother! James's book might be short, but it is powerful, and it sounds a whole lot like what Jesus taught in the Sermon on the Mount (Matthew 5–7). What does James say is the evidence of our faith? Highlight your evidence.

A Temple

Don't you yourselves know that you are God's
temple and that the Spirit of God lives in you?
1 Corinthians 3:16

What does your dream home look like? Have you thought about it before? Is it modern or old-fashioned? In a subdivision, big city, or the country?

It is not hard for me to imagine my dream home. It is quaint and old-fashioned—old homes are my jam. It is on the outskirts of town. I might choose to remodel it to make it my own. It has two stories, a large front porch, and it sits on a few acres of land surrounded by trees and a small creek in the backyard. I would have a home office with built-in bookshelves so tall I would need a sliding ladder. Outside is a back porch, flowers, and a fenced-in garden. Can you see it?

Years ago, God designed an immaculate home where he could dwell, or live, with his people. It was almost perfect—the garden of Eden. People brought sin into the garden, though, so we could not dwell there anymore.

But God was not done meeting with his people; eventually, he instructed his people (the Israelites) to build another place called a temple. It was beautiful, full of gold, precious stones, and intricate architecture. It was the place where God dwelled, and the people could go

to the temple to worship God and talk or pray to him. But God's people could not just come into the temple as they pleased. They had to go to the temple to offer sacrifices for their sins. These sacrifices never fully paid for or wiped away their sins. They covered them until they could be paid in full by Jesus.

Once Jesus, who was God in the flesh, came to earth, died on the cross for our sins, and came back to life, making us right with God, things changed. God moved out of the temple and into his people.

First Corinthians 3:16 says that God lives in his people. God could dwell anywhere, and he chooses his people (the church)! The Holy Spirit lives in the heart of every Christian, and not only does he live in you, but he is also making you more like Jesus! Think of it as a remodel. (The Bible calls this sanctification.) One day soon, all God's children will move into a new, forever home with him.

Until then, remember, you are a temple—a dwelling place for God.

In Case You Want to . . .

Reflect

1. Have you ever thought about God living in you? How does that make you feel?

2. What are some ways you do not treat your heart as God's temple?

3. How does knowing you are a dwelling place for God change the way you live in your life?

Thank God for making his home in you. Ask him to keep remodeling your heart to make you more like him.

Keep Reading

Read John 14:18–26. In this passage, Jesus is talking to his disciples shortly before his crucifixion, his death on the cross. He gives his followers some final instructions and encouragement. Highlight verse 20. In your own words, what does Jesus say in this verse? Who is in him? Who is in us?

An Influencer

Be self-controlled in everything. Make yourself an example
of good works with integrity and dignity in your teaching.
Titus 2:6–7

Before vacationing with our family this summer, my youngest rattled off a list of the twenty things we *must* do at our destination. She was twelve. What does she know about things we *must* do on vacation?

Turns out, she knows a lot. Her favorite YouTube channel gave her an unbelievably detailed list. And wouldn't you know it? Those tips were amazing. Now I *am* obsessed with that YouTuber. I spent an hour folding laundry while her channel kept me company. I have officially been influenced by the influencer.

From everyone dressing like Britney Spears in the '90s to social media stars telling us what to buy next, "influencing" is not new. Companies scan social accounts, looking to promote their products in exchange for discounts, commissions, and freebies. That sounds like a sweet deal to me!

Believe it or not, I am also an influencer. Not because I authored this book, but because God said so. He said so about you too.

You are an influencer.

God calls Christians to influence people. He says in Matthew 28:19–20, "Go, therefore, and make disciples of all nations, baptizing

them in the name of the Father and of the Son and of the Holy Spirit, teaching them to observe everything I have commanded you."

We exist to love God, love others, and tell people about him with our lives and words. He says the way we follow him *influences* the world around us. Our words and actions make a difference in the lives of others. Proverbs 18:21 says our words are life or death, and Titus 2:7 reminds us to do "good works with integrity and dignity." For better or worse, positive or negative, we are influencing. We can speak kind words or hateful ones. We can help someone in need or ignore them. We can show someone undeserving love or disrespect.

How we influence, for good or bad, represents or misrepresents God. So, *how* are you influencing? Is it for God? Is it for yourself? Is it for someone other than God?

Remember, we are God's influencers in the world—let's do our job well.

In Case You Want to . . .

Reflect

1. Is it difficult to believe you are an influencer? Why or why not?

2. In what ways have you positively or negatively influenced those around you?

3. How can you better influence the world? Are you being the kind of influencer God wants you to be? If not, how can you start?

Pray, asking God to show you how you are influencing others and to help you honor him through your influence.

Keep Reading

Read Matthew 5:13–16 and 43–48. In verses 13–16, he says his followers should be like salt and light. How do salt and light make things better? In verses 43–48 Jesus tells his followers to love others. How does loving others influence or affect them?

Alive

But God, who is rich in mercy, because of his great love
that he had for us, made us alive with Christ even though
we were dead in trespasses. You are saved by grace!
Ephesians 2:4–5

I cradled my popcorn and watched the movie through slits of my buttery fingers. Scary movies are *not* my thing. My imagination is active enough. My friends know this, so when they invited me to see a movie with them, I agreed. The story line had me glued, but when the zombies made their appearance, my hands shot over my eyes.

I watched through trembling fingers. In the movie, a virus spreads worldwide, turning people into flesh-eating zombies. They were alive and dead at the same time—no cure for this disease. Eventually, the main character discovers a cure in his blood. He gives his life to save the world. Sound familiar?

The zombie movie was pure fiction, but its themes were not. In the garden of Eden, sin infected humanity. We have no cure for this disease.

We are like zombies—people walking around dead. In Ephesians 2:4–5, the word *trespasses* means any way we have wronged God. We cannot fix ourselves. After the first people God created disobeyed him, sin entered our bloodline. Every human born since Adam and Eve

is cursed by sin. Sin separates us from God forever, and the Bible calls us "dead" in our sins.

Romans 6:23 tells us the payment for sin is death, but the gift of God is eternal life. God sent Jesus into the world as a different kind of person—fully God and fully human.

He is the only human to never be infected by sin. He lived a perfect, fully alive life before he sacrificed himself so that we can be fully alive too. We were dead in our sins, but followers of Jesus are brought back to life! We are alive! The cure to our sin problem is Jesus's sacrifice to save the world, to fix what sin has broken. We do not have to fear death anymore as if it were a scary zombie movie. If you are a follower of Jesus, sin no longer has power over you in this life or the next.

Remember, we are alive in Christ!

In Case You Want to ...

Reflect

1. Why is sin such a big problem?

2. How has God "cured" our sin problem?

3. Adam and Eve brought sin into the world, and it cursed us all. God did not have to find a way to fix it. Why do you believe he did? (Hint: read 1 John 4:9 and John 3:16.)

God loves the world so much that he made a way for us to be with him forever. Because of this, we learn how good, kind, loving, and merciful God is. Thank him for his goodness.

Keep Reading

Read Colossians 2:6–15. What do these verses remind Jesus's followers about being "alive"? Highlight your evidence. How does your life change because of Jesus's sacrifice?

6

Given Purpose

*Mankind, he has told each of you what is good and
what it is the LORD requires of you: to act justly, to love
faithfulness, and to walk humbly with your God.*
Micah 6:8

It was a tie! Another girl and I had been declared the Valentine's Day Queens at the dance. My friends swarmed me, and we cheered and chatted as the music played. Sixth-grade dances are less about dancing and more about socializing. There I was, in a social circle with the cool kids. I could not believe it—I was one of them! That's when I saw Sam. She was not in the popular crowd. In fact, most people made fun of her. But I was always kind to her . . . when no one else was around.

She stood against the back wall, all alone, until she saw me and started walking my way. *Oh no.* I was terrified my friends would see me talking to her! I looked around, but there was nowhere to hide. My friends all sneered as she neared.

I knew the right thing to do. I knew how God would want me to respond to her in front of my friends, but at that moment, I chose to sin.

Sam came to congratulate me, but I acted like I did not know her. I even joined in with the others, making fun of her. Tears streamed down her face, and she ran toward the bathroom.

In Micah 6:8, the Israelites failed to do the things God asked of them, and they were acting like they did not know why God was upset with them. A spokesperson (or prophet) for God named Micah reminded them that God had already told them what to do. Micah said their purpose was to do God's will: to do what was right, to show mercy to others, and to depend on God.

Jesus's two greatest commandments in Matthew 22:34–40 echo Micah 6:8: love God and love others. When we love God, that love should overflow into the way we treat people. My love for God was not showing that night I made fun of Sam. I did not do what was right, I was not kind, and I was not humble. I did not use my words for good, and I did not put others before myself (Philippians 2:3).

We were designed to love God and love others—it is our God-given purpose. I was unkind to Sam at that dance. No one would have known that I loved God by the way I treated her. I am so grateful God has forgiven me for that night. I can choose differently from then and now on. I can choose to live in light of God's purpose for my life, and I hope you will too.

Remember, you have a God-given purpose to love God and love others.

In Case You Want to . . .

Reflect

1. Using Matthew 22:34–40 as your guide, write in your own words what our purpose is.

2. How are you acting justly, showing mercy, and walking humbly with God in your everyday life?

3. What do you think it might look like to act justly, to show mercy, and to walk humbly with God each day?

Ask God to help you act justly, show mercy, and walk humbly with him. If there is someone you find difficult to love, tell God. Ask him to help you be loving toward that person even if you do not feel like it.

Keep Reading

Read 1 Corinthians 10:31–33. Write verse 31 on a sticky note or piece of paper and put it somewhere you will see it every day. I usually put Bible verses on my bathroom mirror, microwave, or laptop. What does this verse tell us to do for the glory of God? How does or should this affect the way we work and live?

Capable

I am able to do all things through him who strengthens me.
Philippians 4:13

When Advanced Chemistry turned into an undercover math class involving letters, numbers, and balancing chemical equations, my brain tapped out. *Nope. Get me out of here.*

"Ma'am," I said to my teacher in my most polite voice. "I'm lost." The class chuckled. I did not mean my statement to be funny. I squirmed at my desk and tried to find words. "I . . . I don't understand. This is too hard."

She was a woman known for her no-nonsense approach. "Hannah," she said, arms folded. "Are you capable of doing hard things?"

The answer was yes. I had been through a lot more than this chemistry class in the past. As a little girl, my dad went to jail for several years. I am a daddy's girl, so when he left, I was heartbroken. This season of my life brimmed with suffering, but God helped my family. I watched my mom work hard to make sure my brother and I had what we needed. We trusted God, read the Bible, and followed him to the best of our ability. When it was tempting to be angry with God, he helped us endure.

I stared at my teacher for a long moment and nodded. Her eyes softened a bit, and I knew this was not about chemistry or equations.

She offered me a half smile. "Then you can do *this*." She turned to the class. "All of you can."

Children of God can do hard things. Philippians 4:13 says that, through God, we are capable. Guess what? It is not just passing chemistry or winning a big game we can do. When Paul wrote those words, he was in jail for preaching about Jesus. The Bible teaches that Paul had been beaten, flogged (whipped), shipwrecked, chased out of towns, and nearly killed throughout his ministry, yet he kept going. He endured suffering with God's help. He even said he was content "whether well fed or hungry, whether in abundance or in need. I am able to do all things through him who strengthens me" (Philippians 4:11–13).

Followers of Jesus can go anywhere God calls us, do anything he has asked us to do, and endure whatever hardship comes our way. Whether we are in seasons of suffering, taking Advanced Chemistry, or both, followers of Jesus can do hard things.

Remember, because God enables you, you are capable.

In Case You Want to . . .

Reflect

1. Describe one or two times you had to do something hard. How did it go? What was hard about it?

2. Suffering is not something we would call good, but how do you think God could use suffering for good?

3. Think of a time you felt God calling you to do something hard. How did he help you through that tough time?

If you are going through a hard season, ask God for his strength. Maybe you know someone who is going through something difficult. Pray for God to give them strength.

Keep Reading

Read Deuteronomy 31:1–8. Moses, the leader of Israel, could not go with the people to the land God promised them, so Moses appointed a new leader, Joshua. This land had a lot of big, strong enemies. How did the people feel when they got a new leader? How does God respond to those feelings?

Week 5

"In every way I've shown you that it is necessary to help the weak . . . to remember the words of the Lord Jesus."

Acts 20:35

Chosen

"You did not choose me, but I chose you. I appointed you to go and produce fruit and that your fruit should remain, so that whatever you ask the Father in my name, he will give you. This is what I command you: Love one another."
John 15:16–17

A friend of mine in high school campaigned to be president of our state Beta Club. His slogan was, "Pick me." While it did not seem creative at the time, I was thrilled to cheer him on.

Election day came, and our candidate took the stage. We jumped and cheered over blaring music, but our cheers were silenced at the sight! There was a *giant nose* on the stage—a *dancing*, giant nose! A dancing giant nose *surrounded* by several other dancers wearing nose T-shirts that said, "Pick me." The crowd erupted into laughter, well, most of them did. A few teachers glared. *Some people have no sense of humor.*

Unfortunately, my friend was not picked, and it made both of us a little sad. Being picked for the team or chosen for an award feels nice, and, as nice as it feels to be picked, it feels equally awful not to be chosen.

One person *does* choose us no matter what we bring to the table: Jesus.

In John 15:16 Jesus says, "You did not choose me, but I chose you." Get excited about that! Seriously, let out a cheer! He *picked* us! He *chose* us. He wants us to be with him forever, no matter what!

Jesus continues, saying he assigns his chosen people to go into the world and produce good fruit. He says he will lead those who follow him to do good things. There is also a promise attached to Jesus's words: "Whatever you ask the Father in my name, he will give you." God is not a genie, granting us any wish we want. This verse says that if we are following Jesus, he will help us want what he wants.

Best. News. Ever!

We do not have to put on a show for God to make him like us more. He does not care if we make him laugh or bring amazing talent to the table. God is not electing people because of what we do. He chooses us because he loves us. He makes us more like himself, and he calls us to go into the world and love people as he loves us (John 15:17).

Remember, God has chosen us, and we get the honor of loving others alongside him.

In Case You Want to . . .

Reflect

1. What do you think it means that God has chosen you? How does it make you feel?

2. What kind of "fruit" are you producing in your life right now?

3. In what ways do you love others? In what ways could you love others more?

Thank God for choosing you. Ask him to help you "produce fruit" throughout your life. Loving others might seem easy, but sometimes it is difficult. We get to choose to love others. Ask God to help you love others the way he loves them.

Keep Reading

Read Luke 15:1–7. Is the man in the story forced to find his sheep, or does he choose to leave and find it? How is the man in the story like God?

Saved

If you confess with your mouth, "Jesus is Lord," and believe in your heart that God raised him from the dead, you will be saved.
Romans 10:9

I could not stand the thought of one more innocent chick dying. How could my family be so cruel? How could I be so cruel? We cracked eggs and scrambled them with a pinch of salt and butter alongside toast and a slice or two of bacon. They were delicious. I despised and adored each bite. *What is wrong with me?*

I was determined to change. I would save these babies from the certain destruction of our ravenous appetites. I thought of the unhatched chicks, and I knew it had to be done. My eight-year-old mind concocted a plan.

While everyone was getting ready, I snuck into the kitchen, pulled a few eggs from the refrigerator, and swooped them off to the safety of our barn. Day after day, I saved a few more eggs. Mom scratched her head each morning as she went to the fridge, wondering aloud about where the eggs were. I kept quiet and held my head low so as not to make eye contact. My silence was saving chicks by the day.

Eventually, Mom discovered my covert operation. Though she was not angry, she kindly explained the difference between eggs we eat and eggs that hatch into chicks. *What a relief!*

Sin, which is anything that goes against God's words, entered the world and separated humanity from God. We are sinners. But God loves people so much that he made a way for us to be with him again. He had a plan! He sent his perfect Son Jesus to pay the price for our sins. Jesus conquered sin by living a life of perfect obedience to God, dying on the cross, and rising from the dead on the third day!

He says anyone who believes in him will be saved—meaning, he lives in every one of his followers now, and one day he will live among us again! If your identity is in Jesus, you are saved from sin to a life with him! Talk about putting our eggs all in one basket.

Romans 10:9 says that if you recognize Jesus as Lord, or the leader, of your life, and if you believe God brought him from death to life, you will be saved! Saved from what? Sin and its punishment of eternal separation from God. Deciding to make Jesus the Lord of your life means choosing to be like him every day, doing the things he did and asked us to do.

My mission to save the baby chickens failed, but remember, God's mission to save you and me did not.

In Case You Want to . . .

Reflect

1. Based on Romans 10:9, explain what it means to be "saved."

2. Have you been saved? If so, write about how or when you chose to completely trust Jesus with your life.

Thank God for making a way for us to be with him again through Jesus's sacrifice. If you have faith in Jesus, you have been saved. Ask God to help you follow Jesus by doing the things he asks you to do.

Keep Reading

Read Romans 10:1–13. Based on what you have read in these Scriptures, who can be saved? How are they saved? Do you think this is good news for people? Why or why not? If you think it is good news, who could you share it with? Write their names down and ask God to give you a chance to share this good news with them.

Comforted

He comforts us in all our affliction, so that we may be able to comfort those who are in any kind of affliction, through the comfort we ourselves receive from God.
2 Corinthians 1:4

Clothes, fresh and warm from the dryer, sat on the couch waiting to be folded. When I was a child, this was an open invitation.

The morning was cool, and chill bumps prickled my arms and legs. I hurried to the couch and jumped onto the pile, wiggling and cocooning myself in the warmth. The clean, honeysuckle scent of laundry soap engulfed me. I smiled and burrowed deeper. *Sweet comfort.* Mom folded them around me. I basked in the middle of her daily chore, but she did not mind my presence. It made her smile.

As a mom, I want to pass little comforts like this on to my own children. When they were little, I would heat their blankets or pajamas in the dryer. They would sigh, smile, and melt beneath the warm covers. When the dryer buzzed, they would come running to the living room, waiting for me to drop the pile onto the couch so that they could cuddle beside the clothes. I did not mind. It made me smile.

Comfort looks different for each of us. For some, it is a cup of hot cocoa, a favorite blanket, a baggy shirt, or a homey place. But our word for comfort comes from the Latin *comfortare,* which means to

strengthen greatly. The prefix *com-* means "together or with," and *-fort* refers to "something strong"—think of a military fort. Paul writes in 2 Corinthians 1:4 that God comforts us. As Paul preached about Jesus, he endured much suffering—beatings, shipwrecks, imprisonment, and poverty. His life hardly seemed comfortable. Yet he taught that God comforts us.

When Paul says God comforts followers of Jesus, he means so much more than providing us with ease and relaxation or a pile of cozy warm clothes. When God comforts his children, he is with us, strengthening us greatly!

God does not say we will not have troubles. He says we *will* have troubles, but that he has overcome the world (John 16:33)! When we are uncomfortable, God does not waste our struggles. He works them out for good (Romans 8:28). He comforts us by giving us strength to do his will, consoling us, giving us rest, and having compassion for us.

A warm pile of laundry or hot cocoa might relax us for a moment, but remember, God's comfort strengthens us for a lifetime!

In Case You Want to . . .

Reflect

1. What things bring relaxation? What about comfort?

2. How does the definition of comfort change the way you think about God's comfort?

3. How has God comforted you?

God strengthens his children. He comforts them. When he comforts you, thank him. Ask him to help you know how to comfort others who are in need.

Keep Reading

Read 2 Corinthians 1:3–7. Paul talks a lot about comfort in this passage. How many times do you see the word *comfort*? What do you learn about God and comfort through the passage?

A Friend

"I do not call you servants anymore, because a servant doesn't know what his master is doing. I have called you friends, because I have made known to you everything I have heard from my Father."
John 15:15

Why is this so difficult? I grunted and whined as I pried my eye open with my fingers, trying—with surgeon-like precision—to get my contact to go on my eyeball correctly! But my eye had a brain of its own. It refused to cooperate. *Sigh.* Contacts were a new thing in college-Hannah's life, and she did not love them.

I had a friend who would help me get them in. But could I call her . . . *again*? I looked at my clock. Classes started in thirty minutes. *No time to waste.* I grabbed my phone, called her, and in no time, she was at my doorstep with a smile, ready and willing to touch my eyeball. There is *nothing* like a good friend.

Friends are the best. When I was a preschooler, my friends and I played pretend together. In elementary school, my friends and I played sports together. As preteens, we survived puberty together. When I was a teenager, my friends navigated the road to adulthood alongside me.

Through each age and stage of my life, friends have been by my side, from sleeping over and enjoying girls' nights out to enduring tough times. Sometimes, friends grow apart during life's changing seasons, or

they part ways for other reasons. Even now I love my girls! I trust them. I like them. I want to be around them. I can count on them. They are my sisters. We have each other's backs.

In John 15:15, Jesus says we are his friends. I don't know about you, but sometimes I find that hard to understand. Jesus is my Lord, my Savior, the boss of my life, but my *friend*? *What?* That seems so hard to believe. You and I are big sinners. Why would he want to be our friend?

Jesus chooses friendship with us because he loves us! He does not love us because of anything we do—he loves us just because he wants to. He does not grow apart from us when seasons change, and he never parts ways with us for any reason at all.

He does not put your contacts in, but friendship with him is better than any friendship we have on earth. Being his friend means we can trust him, talk to him whenever we want, and believe he will never leave us.

Remember, you have the best friend ever in Jesus!

In Case You Want to . . .

Reflect

1. Think of a time when you were a good friend. How is Jesus a better friend?

2. Think of a time when you were a bad friend. How can you look to Jesus as an example of how to do better?

3. How does knowing Jesus is your friend influence your friendships with others?

Friendship is a gift from God. Take a few moments to thank God for the friends in your life and for his friendship. If you are struggling to find meaningful friendships, talk with God about it. Thank him for being a good friend.

Keep Reading

Read John 15:9–17. This doesn't mean he *will* be our friend if we obey him enough, but that our obedience to him is *proof* that we are his friends. What does he command us to do? (Hint: read verse 12.) In what ways do you think Jesus shows his love for us?

5

A Champion

The LORD advances like a warrior; he stirs up his zeal like a soldier. He shouts, he roars aloud, he prevails over his enemies.

Isaiah 42:13

Pull!" I yelled and gritted my teeth.

Grunts sounded in unison.

My hands gripped the rope tighter as my homeroom lined up behind me and held onto it. I did not mind how the rope made my palms burn. We would be insanely sore the next day. Some might pull a muscle. *So be it.* "Tug-of-War Champ" was a highly sought-after title, and our class was going to win, no matter the cost.

I took *the* stance—knees slightly bent, feet apart, with one in front of the other. Then I sat back and used the strength of my legs to pull. Everyone else did the same. The enemy class—I mean, the opposing class—lurched forward as we tugged. I saw the struggle in their eyes, and it spurred me on.

"Keep going!" I dug my heels into the gym floor and ignored my throbbing palms. "Pull! We can do it!"

We tugged and pulled. Grunts and groans grew louder, and inch by inch our efforts moved the other team closer and closer to the line until . . .

We yanked them across! Our class erupted in cheers. We were one stop closer to being the champs!

Because of Jesus's sacrifice and God's defeat of Satan, we *are not* playing tug-of-war. Isaiah 42:13 reminds us God prevails over the enemy!

God has already fought the war for us and won! We are not fighting the match that decides if God or Satan wins. God has already fought and won, and we get the "highly sought-after" title of being on the champion team! Romans 8:37 says it like this: "In all these things we are more than conquerors through him who loved us."

Because of Jesus, we are more than conquerors. We are on God's team—the winning team! And with every kind word, display of generosity, and act of selflessness, we get the privilege of reflecting Jesus the Champion-King.

Our homeroom lost the last tug-of-war match. *Heartbreaking.* But there is no loss if you are on God's team.

Remember, when we are on God's team, we are champions!

In Case You Want to . . .

Reflect

1. Have you ever thought about children of God being "champions"? How does this make you feel, or what does it make you think of?

2. List a few reasons why knowing that God prevails over Satan is important.

3. How does knowing God wins in the end change your life today?

God wants you to join him in his good work. Thank God for the privilege of being on his champion team. Ask him to show you how he wants you to live like you are on his team.

Keep Reading

Read Colossians 3:12–17. Think about it. What are these verses asking followers of Jesus to do? How does this passage remind you that God wins?

So Loved

"For God loved the world in this way: He gave his one and only Son, so that everyone who believes in him will not perish but have eternal life."
John 3:16

I love you this much," my son said. My toddler's chubby arms stretched to each side. I straightened his pajama top and helped him hop into bed.

"Well, I love you this much." I stretched my arms wider.

He bobbed his head as if he were impressed by my expression of love for him, but then he grinned.

"Oh yeah?" he said, hopping on his bed, hands on his hips. "Well, I love you this much!" His voice went up an octave, and he strained, widening his arms as far as he could. He groaned and grimaced, face reddening, chest out, and arms back.

"Wow! That is a whole big bunch, kiddo." I laughed and scooped him up. We argued back and forth like this until it was time for prayers and lights out.

I knew my arms were longer than his, though he did not seem to notice. I loved him deeper than his little mind could comprehend. Now, though he is nearly grown and his arm span is wider than mine, I *still* love him more. I may not be able to scoop him up, but I *so* love that boy of mine. He is my son.

God loves us more than that. We may say to him, "I love you this much," and stretch our arms as far as we can, but God loves us so much that he sent his only Son to stretch his arms out on a cross and die for sins we deserve to die for. Our sin did not stop him from loving us! Romans 5:8 says, "But God proves his own love for us in that while we were still sinners, Christ died for us." *Wow.* That is a big love.

God loves you more than you love him even when you read your Bible every day. His affection for you is deeper than yours feels—even when your heart swells during worship. When it feels like he is nowhere near, he loves you more than you can comprehend. In some ways, you and I are like toddlers trying to outdo our confession of love to God.

We may say, "I love you more," but remember, you and I can never out-love our God.

In Case You Want to . . .

Reflect

1. Do you feel loved by God? Why or why not?

2. Have you ever felt like you love God more than he loves you? Why did or do you feel that way?

3. How does knowing you are loved by God change the way you want to live your life?

Take a moment and think about how much God loves you. Thank him for loving you. If you do not feel his love, remember our feelings do not make something true or untrue. Ask God to help you trust that you are loved.

Keep Reading

Read 1 John 4:16–21. In verse 16, God is described as love. God *is* love. List three things these verses teach you about God and love.

Enduring

"But the one who endures to the end will be saved."
Matthew 24:13

Six to eight weeks in a cast was basically a lifetime—all because of a trampoline. It is possible nothing hurts worse than armpits rubbed raw by crutches' "cushions" and the throbbing blisters that appear between your thumb and pointer finger from holding on to the handles. Oh, and do not forget the ankle, which is in a cast, toes dangling out in the open. It is a whole ordeal.

Not only did my ankle hurt, but I could not do everyday things I loved. No PE. Taking a bath or shower was complicated. And I lost two or three pencils down the cast in attempts to ease the itchiness. To this day I refuse to jump on trampolines, or as I call them, ankle-breaking deathtraps. The whole experience was a test of endurance.

Life can be challenging, but you and I are called to endure. We are asked to do harder things than wearing a cast for weeks. In Matthew 24:13, Jesus answers a question about how his followers would know he was coming back. He says, "You are going to hear of wars and rumors of wars. See that you are not alarmed, because these things must take place, but the end is not yet" (Matthew 24:6). He describes famine, earthquakes, and people *hating* Jesus's followers. Jesus says those who endure are his true followers. They are the ones who belonged

to him in the first place. Our endurance, even in challenging times, is evidence of our faith in Jesus!

We will face difficulties in our lives. If you have not already been through hard times, they will come. Sometimes difficulties happen because of our poor choices. They are consequences. Other times, we might be affected by other people's bad choices. Sometimes terrible things just happen because this world is broken and full of sin. In John 16:33, Jesus says we will have trouble in this life but that we should be courageous because he has conquered the world. Because of Jesus, we can endure the hard things!

Enduring might mean resisting temptation when everyone else around you is not. It could mean sharing the good news of Jesus with a friend even though they might reject your words. Or enduring might be choosing joy and kindness when you are inclined to be negative.

God is always with us, and Jesus has overcome the world! When we are broken and doing our best to hobble along, remember, we can endure.

In Case You Want to . . .

Reflect

1. Have you had to endure something difficult in your life? Write about it.

2. Did you see God working in that difficulty? If so, how?

3. Hard times are no fun. How does knowing God calls us to endure influence your life?

Thank God for helping you endure challenging times. Ask him to use those times to teach you something new about him. Ask God to show you someone to encourage because of the lessons you have learned.

Keep Reading

Read 2 Corinthians 4:1–18. Highlight any verses that remind you how to endure difficulty. Read verses 16–18 again. Why are we not to give up? What is being produced or made in us? How does this make you feel?

Week 6

I remember the days of old; I meditate on all you have done; I reflect on the work of your hands.
Psalm 143:5

Treasured

*"For you are a holy people belonging to the L*ord *your God.*
*The L*ord *your God has chosen you to be his own possession*
out of all the peoples on the face of the earth."
Deuteronomy 7:6

Over one hundred of them had to be lined up along the wall of our barn loft. They sparkled like diamonds when the light hit them right. They were not diamonds. They were more valuable—to me, at least. My rock collection—geode collection, to be exact—was my treasure.

I grew up close to Mammoth Cave in Kentucky. It is the largest cave system in the world, and I loved visiting it. Our summer vacations usually included an excursion through the caves and the little nearby shops that sold geodes from the caves. Geodes shine. They are colorful. They sparkle and twinkle like jewels in a treasure box.

I built my collection until middle school, lining each new addition in the "hidden" spot of our barn. They were my most valued possession.

The truth was, they were not valuable. They were rocks. Simple rocks. Cheap rocks. Not a treasure to anyone except me.

Do you ever think of yourself that way—plain and simple, not an especially valuable person? That is not true. Go back to the first devotion and remind yourself that you have value because you are made in the image of God. Next, if you are a child of God, Deuteronomy tells you that

you are his own possession. Some versions of Deuteronomy 7:6 say you are his "treasured" possession.

His treasures cannot be snatched from his hand (John 10:28). You are his; you are "remarkably and wondrously made" (Psalm 139:14). God rejoices over his children with gladness and delights with singing (Zephaniah 3:17)! Imagine God crafting you carefully like the expert designer he is and then singing and cheering because he treasures you that much! We are his treasures.

We may not feel like treasures, but try to rest in God's truth. Whether you feel it or not, you have worth.

My geodes were my treasures. Someone else may have looked at them and called them worthless, but they were priceless to me. They were mine. They were cared for and loved. How much more does God love his children? He says it in his very own words. In his eyes, you shine brighter than any geode or jewel.

Remember, you are his treasure.

In Case You Want to . . .

Reflect

1. Think about your greatest treasure on earth. Is it something that has a lot of value? Is it a person? How does it make you feel that God treasures you infinitely more?

2. How does knowing you are treasured by God change the way you live?

Thank God that he treasures you and all his people. Ask God to help you treasure others as he does.

Keep Reading

Read Psalm 139:13–16. In this psalm, the psalmist praises God for making him with such great care and detail. How does the way God formed you show how much he treasures you?

Never Alone

"And remember, I am with you always, to the end of the age."
Matthew 28:20

It hurt to watch them leave, and it hurt to willingly stay behind. It hurt to sit alone in the college dorm room and know my life would never be the same. Growing up, graduating high school, and moving out of my family home felt . . . bad. I knew this next step was a good thing. I was the first person in my family to go to college, but it still felt hard. Part of me mourned the loss of childhood and the comforts of home. I feared the answer to the question "What's next?" Yet another part of me bubbled with excitement. *Finally, I am an adult!* Still, I sat on the edge of my dorm room bed and ugly cried.

I grabbed a box of tissues from the nightstand as my nose turned into Niagara Falls and tears spilled down my cheeks. For the first time, I was on my own. I felt alone. I buried my face in a pillow and cried harder.

In Matthew 28, Jesus had come back to life! Just weeks before, he had been murdered by a mob and the Roman government, buried in a tomb, and risen from the dead. He spent the next few weeks appearing to his followers so that they would know he was alive! He appeared to the women who followed him, and he appeared to his eleven disciples, telling them to go tell others he was alive! He later gave them a job to

do. We call it "The Great Commission." Jesus told them to make followers of Jesus in all nations.

This job assignment was huge! Go and make disciples of *all* nations? Teach them to do *everything* Jesus commanded? The disciples must have felt overwhelmed by such a massive task. They might even have felt all alone, left to do this challenging thing all by themselves. Jesus said, "And remember, I am with you always, to the end of the age." Even though Jesus was getting ready to leave their physical side, he promised he would be with his followers always. They would never be alone.

This promise is not only for his original disciples but also for us who follow Jesus now. He is with us. We are never alone. It is true no person was in the room with me on my first day of college life, but I was not alone. God had called me, a young college student, into a new season where he would give me the opportunity to make disciples. Whatever task or job he puts in our paths, we are not doing it alone.

Whether we are sitting in a dorm room for the first time, entering a new stage of life, or feeling alone—remember, he is with us always.

In Case You Want to . . .

Reflect

1. Describe a time you felt alone.

2. How does knowing God was with you during that time make you feel?

3. Write the last portion of Matthew 28:20 beginning with the word *And*. Then circle the word *you*. Next, write your name to the side of that circle.

God is with you, no matter where you are, how you are feeling, or what is going on in your life. Thank God for being with you. Ask him to help you remember he is always there.

Keep Reading

Read John 14:15–26. Jesus told his followers right before he died that the Father would send someone to be with them forever. Who would God send? Where would that person be? Why is this a good or beneficial thing? If you are a follower of God, he is with you. You are never alone.

A New Creation

Therefore, if anyone is in Christ, he is a new creation; the
old has passed away, and see, the new has come!
2 Corinthians 5:17

There is something soothing about sipping an iced coffee, strolling down the antique mall aisles, and browsing the items in each booth. It takes time and a little digging, but I love it. My mind wanders as I touch the objects, turn them over in my hands, and imagine the story the little treasures hold.

On one antique mall outing, I discovered several old plates covered in dust. The plates were assorted sizes, and each had a distinct color and pattern. Dingy, dented, and dull candlesticks were tossed in a box close to the plates. *Hmmm.*

I took my tainted treasures home and imagined endless possibilities before settling on the best. With a little soap and water, paint, and glue, I crafted several adorable makeup and jewelry stands. I even gave some away as gifts! *Winning.*

Give me rust and chipped paint, and make sure it is tossed aside, broken, bent, dented, and dingy. Dilapidated barns—yes, please! That fixer-upper starter home—bring it on. Someone else's trash is my treasure.

The junk pile can be a place to find those chic, shabby, trendy items. I love this concept. There is something redeeming, deep, and strangely familiar about taking something old and making it new.

It is what God did for us. He looked at humanity after we tainted ourselves with sin. We are dirty, dented, and distressed, but he saw potential. He saw what we could be with him, and he made a way for us to be new.

He picked his kids up and turned us into his new creations. We are more than refurbished; we are new. Second Corinthians 5:17 says it best: "Therefore, if anyone is in Christ, he is a new creation; the old has passed away, and see, the new has come!"

Anyone who follows Jesus is a new creation. Jesus forgives our sins and makes us more like him. He gives us new hearts that want the things he wants. This transformation is an ongoing process. Followers of Jesus will not be perfect until we have been raised from the dead and all things are set right, but even before that, he makes us new!

Remember, in Christ, you are a new creation, treasured by God!

In Case You Want to . . .

Reflect

1. Has God given you a new heart through Jesus's death and resurrection? If so, what is the story?

2. How does it make you feel to know you have been made new in Jesus?

Thank God for loving you even as a sinner. If you have decided to follow him, thank him for making you a new creation. Ask him to help you follow him for the rest of your life.

Keep Reading

Read Colossians 3:1–10. What happens when God makes us new?

A Kingdom Citizen

When I was in the sixth grade, our house burned down. It was a couple of weeks after Christmas. Praise God, my brother and I were at school, and Mom and Dad had gone to work. None of my family was home when the fire started. Though the firefighters tried, the house could not be saved. We lost almost everything.

Middle school is hard enough without losing your safest place or experiencing emotional and financial trauma with your family. Thankfully, our community rallied to meet our needs. For a while, we stayed with my granny in accommodations that could hardly be described as roomy, but we were grateful for her help. Eventually, we rented a little farmhouse near our original home while we endured the challenging process of rebuilding. It took for-ev-er.

We were *not* living our best lives, that is for sure. Nothing felt like home. I missed my bed and my pillow. I missed my clothes. I missed the comforts of my house. I longed for this trial to be over and to be back in my home. I hated the in-between.

You and I are living in between homes. This world is not our forever home. We are temporary citizens of this planet and these countries,

states, cities, and neighborhoods. Our *real* citizenship is in God's kingdom, meaning, even though you live on earth, God is the ruler of your life. One day, God will bring heaven and earth together, make them completely new and perfect, and his kingdom will become a physical place where there will be . . .

No tears.

No pain.

Only joy.

God's children will spend eternity celebrating, feasting, and praising him. We will perfectly love God and others. It is the place you are made for, the place that feels like home, the place where your citizenship is.

Check out how Jesus prays for us in John 17: "They are not of the world, just as I am not of the world" (v. 16), and "I want those you have given me to be with me where I am" (v. 24).

You are already a citizen of God's kingdom, and Jesus made a way for you to be there with him one day! God makes you a native of his kingdom. You can live like you belong there by loving God and loving others with your words and actions. And one day, God will bring you to your safest place—his home.

Remember, Jesus said, "If I go away and prepare a place for you, I will come again and take you to myself, so that where I am you may be also" (John 14:3).

In Case You Want to . . .

Reflect

1. Have you ever felt like you do not belong? Explain.

2. How do you feel knowing your real home is in God's kingdom?

3. How does knowing this change the way you live your life?

Thank God for giving you a forever home in heaven with him. Spend some time imagining what the new heaven and earth will be like! Whatever you imagine, it will be even better!

Keep Reading

Read Ephesians 2:13–21. Read verse 19 again. Highlight it. Followers of God are fellow citizens and members of whose household? How does one become a citizen? (Hint: read verse 13.)

Secure

"I give them eternal life, and they will never perish.
No one will snatch them out of my hand."
John 10:28

Those passing by said it was the scariest roller coaster they had ever ridden. One guy said he would never get on it again. Another said she thought she was going to die. *Gulp.*

So why was I standing in line? *Double gulp.* Because I like thrill rides? *I do.* Because it would be fun? *Hopefully.* Because I was with friends who wanted to ride? *I cannot chicken out.* Because I had waited an hour already? *Yes.* Besides, if this ride was not safe and secure, it would be shut down. *Right?* My palms sweated. My breathing shallowed. I cleared my throat and sucked in a heap of air, doing my best to make small talk with my friends. *Keep cool. Keep calm. Laugh a little.* What was I so afraid of?

Standing in line, I pulled my phone out and started typing in to my search bar. *Whew.* No one had been hurt—on *this* ride. The search brought up hundreds of other articles about roller coasters and injuries. My chest tightened. *Dear Lord, help me!* I clicked my phone off and tucked it into my beloved '90s fanny pack. It was too late to go back. Our time arrived, and before I knew it, I was locked into a seat. *Ready or not.*

The engineers who designed this roller coaster spent countless hours perfecting the tiniest details. A team of professionals built it piece by piece. I had a choice to make. I could trust the ones who made this ride or not. I could trust it was secure, or I could panic.

Faith can be like a scary roller coaster. We wonder if God will really hold on to us. Are our doubts too big? Will Jesus change his mind about us? Will we sin so much that God does not want us anymore? There are unseen twists, turns, ups, and downs on our walks with God. Sometimes a loop comes your way. Sometimes it will feel like you are falling backward. But no matter what, you are secure with Jesus. Nothing can shake you out of his hand. God is like the roller coaster engineer, but better. Jesus reminds us of our security in John 10:28. He says he holds his people in his hand. No one can snatch them away. He is the expert engineer, and we are safe in his grip.

I survived the ride. It was, in fact, the scariest ride ever. Yes, I squealed and screamed as the wind distorted my terrified face. We are safe and secure with Jesus on our best and worst days. Remember, he has you. You can trust him with your life—past, present, and future, here on earth and in heaven.

And even in the line for a roller coaster.

In Case You Want to . . .

Reflect

1. Are you experiencing any "roller-coaster" moments in your life right now? If so, what are they?

2. Do you ever wonder if Jesus will change his mind about you? Why?

3. What can you do when you, friends, or family pull to the same line "roller-coaster" moments?

Ask God to remind you that you are secure. Thank him for keeping you safe in his hands. Take a moment to pray for others you know who need the same prayer. Ask God to remind them that they are secure.

Keep Reading

Read Acts 16:16–40. What difficulties did Paul and Silas face? Write them down. Even though they endured hardships, how did God keep them secure?

Unified

*For just as the body is one and has many parts, and all the parts
of that body, though many, are one body—so also is Christ.
For we were all baptized by one Spirit into one body—whether
Jews or Greeks, whether slaves or free—and we were all given
one Spirit to drink. Indeed, the body is not one part but many.*
I Corinthians 12:12–14

Group projects. *Ugh.*

I almost felt you roll your eyes with me. Or maybe you clapped your hands. It really depends on what kind of group member you are. Do you help in the planning and preparation, pull your own weight? Or do you find yourself on the outskirts, not knowing your group role? You may deal with personality conflicts between those who argue about who is in charge or the one who contributes nothing but is happy to accept an awesome grade (do not be that person). *Sheesh.* Sometimes it is easier to go solo. There *are* benefits to group projects, though, like dividing the workload, sharing ideas, seeing other perspectives, and having accountability partners.

For that sliver of time, part of your identity is wrapped up in a group. During the project, the group is one. *You* are unified.

Like a much better kind of group project, followers of Jesus are all one. We learn in 1 Corinthians 12:13–14 that our identity in Christ is wrapped up in the unity of believers. *We* are unified.

And when we focus on *me* . . .

And forget about *we* . . .

We miss this key component of our identity.

Our identity in Christ is personal, but it is not private. It is individual, but it is not isolated. The Bible calls the community of all Christians "the church," and there is no Christian in the Bible who is not part of the church. Community with other Christ-followers is baked into God's beautiful plan.

Our unity with other believers matters. This "group project" is our common mission to love God, love people, and tell others about Jesus.

Jesus prayed for our unity in John 17:22–23: "I have given them the glory you [God the Father] have given me, so that they may be one as we are one. I am in them, and you are in me, so that they may be made completely one."

The way we love each other shows the world who Jesus is. Our group project lets everyone know that God sent Jesus.

Remember, our unity with other believers brings us closer to God.

In Case You Want to . . .

Reflect

1. What does it mean that your identity as a Christian is wrapped up with others? How does that fact change your life?

2. What kind of "group" member have you been in the church?

3. If the way we love each other shows the world who God is, what happens when we are hateful toward each other? How does that impact the "group project"?

Ask God to help you remember that you belong to the church. Pray for what Jesus prayed for—the unity of all believers so that the world will know that God sent Jesus.

Keep Reading

Read 1 Corinthians 12:20–13:13. Did you know this passage is about love for the church? How does chapter 12 change the way you read chapter 13?

Called and Commissioned

"Go, therefore, and make disciples of all nations, baptizing them in the name of the Father and of the Son and of the Holy Spirit, teaching them to observe everything I have commanded you. And remember, I am with you always, to the end of the age."
Matthew 28:19–20

Before leaving, Jesus gave his disciples instructions on what to do while he was gone—how to spread the good news that Jesus came to earth, died for our sins, and rose again. He asked them to tell the world that everyone can choose to be right with God and spend eternity with him when we die! Jesus told his disciples, "Go." He said to make disciples and teach new believers how to follow him.

That was a command to all believers everywhere.

During a middle school summer camp, I first felt God nudge my heart to "go" too. At the time, I did not know what that meant. What could I do? What kind of ministry? Where? When? How?

As the years passed, God's tug never left me. He called me to be a disciple-maker when I was a kid whose house burned down, a high schooler learning to drive, a scared new college student, a military spouse, a teacher to middle schoolers, a mom, and in every other season of my life. It has been over twenty years since I felt that call. I now serve

on staff at my local church, but the truth is, God has used my whole life as a ministry.

No matter where God calls you to go, a Christian's life is ministry.

You, too, can answer this call to "go" and make disciples. The ways are limitless! Download a Bible app and start a Bible reading plan with a friend or two. Invite friends to church with you. Text a Bible verse or encouraging words to family members as God brings them to your mind. Pray for opportunities to share your faith. Consider starting a Bible study for your friends or go through this devotional with a younger believer. Pray for God to show you how to make disciples in your everyday life.

You might be called to author books, teach history, clean houses, lead a company, walk dogs, or wait tables. In case you forget, you are called and commissioned to go! There is no calling too small to be a ministry.

Remember, Jesus will be with you to the end of the age.

In Case You Want to . . .

Reflect

1. When Jesus calls and commissions his disciples, what does he want them to do?

2. What does that call look like in your life?

3. Has God ever called you to do something? It may be as simple as calling you to follow him. Describe that time.

God gives his followers a big job to do—make disciples! Thank God for inviting you along on a journey to share this good news with everyone! Following him is a great adventure.

Keep Reading

Read 2 Timothy 4:1–5. In Paul's second letter to Timothy, he tells him to do the work of an evangelist. To evangelize simply means to preach the gospel (the good news of Jesus). How do these verses remind you of Jesus's calling and commission of his followers?

Notes